beat
stress
quickly

Terry Looker and Olga Gregson

Hodder Education
338 Euston Road, London NW1 3BH.

Hodder Education is an Hachette UK company

First published in UK 2011 by Hodder Education,

Typeset by Cenveo Publisher Services

Printed in Great Britain by CPI Cox & Wyman, Reading.

Contents

1

what is stress?

Stress is an experience that is part of being human. Each of us creates a state of stress within our self that is unique to each and every one of us.

The state of stress experienced can be defined as particular patterns of emotional and physiological neuronal responses to all the stimulation we experience. A stress pattern occurs when there is a mismatch between what we perceive as demands and our perceived ability to cope with those demands. It is the balance between how we view demands and how we think we can cope with those demands that determines whether we experience stress.

This means that only we as individuals can control and manage our stress. Stress management is a personal, life skill that can be learned. We can all benefit from learning more about stress and how to handle it.

The stress balance

The concept of stress can be illustrated and explained by using a simplified model (Figure 1) which we have called 'the stress balance'.

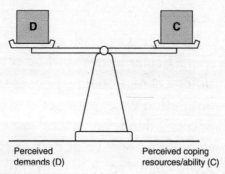

Perceived
demands (D)

Perceived coping
resources/ability (C)

Figure 1 The stress balance.

In the pan on one side of the balance is what we see as the demands (shown as D) around us. In the other pan is what we see as our ability to cope or deal with those demands (shown as C). When we feel able to handle our demands then C will balance D. This does not mean, however, that the scales are necessarily perfectly horizontal. Because we are dealing with a psychological phenomenon, we do not know how much of C is needed to be in total balance with D. We do not necessarily have to have equal weights in each pan in order to be in balance. Rather, the scales should be seen as fluctuating up and down to some degree through a zone of balance, which we will refer to as the 'normal zone' (Figure 2).

The extent of this zone will be different for every individual and indicates that the body is operating in a normal and healthy way. In this zone we would not say we are experiencing stress. The normal zone can be regarded as our everyday living zone, or normal situations zone, in which we are dealing with familiar and routine daily changes in

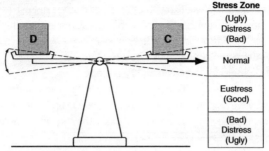

Situation: fluctuations in perceived demands and perceived coping resources but balance remains in the normal stress zone.

Figure 2 The normal zone.

our environment and with everyday demands that, through our experience, we know pose no major threats. Our body adapts to the changing situation by activating our stress response to a degree that we are hardly aware of. In fact, if we were fully conscious of every little change in our body, we would be less effective in dealing with challenges, novel and emergency situations when these arise. So the stress response is always in a low state of activity, held in a state of readiness for further or full activation but without us constantly experiencing stress.

Note: When the term 'stress' is used throughout this book, it refers to any degree of activation of the stress response outside the normal zone, be it either distress or eustress. The activity of the stress response in the normal zone should be considered as an inevitable part of our lives and when in this zone we do not experience 'stress'.

Of course there will be times when small changes in D and C will occur, perhaps as a result of inevitable daily hassles and not feeling too well, so the balance will tip one way and then the other. As long as these fluctuations are within the normal zone of balance, then we would not say we are distressed or eustressed but perhaps we would say we felt a little niggled or stimulated at times. It is when the balance tips outside the normal zone that we experience stress as distress or eustress, and clearly the greater the Imbalance the stronger these feelings will be. Imbalance can occur in two ways:

1 Alterations in perceived nature of demands
2 Changes in perceived ability to cope.

Altering demands may not be easy to achieve, so altering the way we perceive the demand and building up coping skills so we are ready to deal with demands is the shrewd move for managing stress.

Distress

When we face an increased number of demands or view the demands that confront us as difficult or threatening, we need to make a judgement about our ability to cope. If that judgement is 'No, I can't cope', then the stress balance can tip into the distress zone as shown in Figure 3. Having too much to do in too little time; dealing with complex tasks without adequate training; promotion into a job for which we are not suited; having too many bills to pay and not enough income; worrying how we will manage if we lose our job; having domestic problems at the same time as changes at work – these are just a few examples of the kinds of demands that can lead to distress.

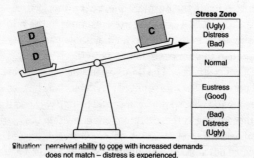

Situation: perceived ability to cope with increased demands does not match – distress is experienced.

Figure 3 The distress zone I.

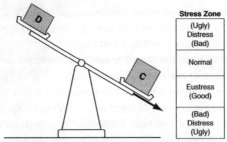

Situation: perceived ability to cope far outweighs the perceived demands; boredom, frustration – distress experienced.

Figure 4 The distress zone II.

Distress can also arise from having too few demands to stimulate you, resulting in boredom and frustration. In this case, perceived ability to cope outweighs demands as shown in Figure 4. Having too little to do or too few demanding tasks can be just as distressful as having too much to do or tackling complex jobs. This situation commonly arises when people retire or are given jobs which do not match their abilities.

Eustress

Eustress can be experienced when our perceived ability to cope outweighs our perceived demands as shown in Figure 5.

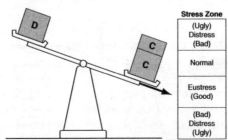

Situation: perceived ability to cope far outweighs the perceived demands; confident, creative – eustress experienced.

Figure 5 The eustress zone.

Although we have an imbalance here, clearly this is a desirable one. In this respect, eustress can be regarded as an extension of the normal zone of the stress balance.

Notice here that the situation is different from that described in Figure 4 where distress results from having too few demands. The eustress situation gives rise to a feeling of confidence, of being in control and able to tackle and handle tasks, challenges and demands. The stress response is activated by just the right amount to provide the alertness, the mental and physical performance required to be productive and creative.

The right balance

Because of the way we live today, we are almost certain to feel distress at some time or another, so we need to reduce the frequency and extent to which the stress balance tips into the distress zones. We can do this by decreasing the number and type of demands and by building up our coping resources. This will help to avoid or minimize the effects of distressful situations. We need to learn how to increase our excursions into the eustress zone by getting the right balance between demands and coping resources.

To get the right balance we need to reappraise how we perceive and interact with our environment because this determines the way we match up our demands with our ability to cope.

We cannot live a life devoid of distress so the important thing is not to allow our stress balance to remain permanently in the distress zone and not to stray into this zone too far and too often. Instead we should aim to use our stress response to improve our lives and performance by keeping our balance in the normal and eustress zones. This can be achieved by learning the skills to alter the balance between demands and coping ability and this is the basis for the effective management of stress.

In order to learn these skills it is necessary to understand how the stress response operates in the body.

The stress response

The term 'stress response' describes a series of different and complex responses made by the body to any demand it faces.

The stress response is always active to some degree, operating within the normal zone of the stress balance to enable us to deal with everyday changes in the environment. When unusual, novel or excessive demands, challenges or threats arise, the stress response ensures that the body is always in a state of readiness to deal with them.

Because demands can be life-threatening, physical, emotional, pleasant or unpleasant, the body's response must be appropriate for dealing with the type of situation faced. It would not be effective and economical for the body to activate a single fixed stress response to deal with all eventualities, so different parts and levels of the stress response are activated to enable us to respond in the most appropriate way.

If we are suddenly confronted by an actual life-threatening situation such as a car hurtling out of control towards us or someone about to attack us, our response must be immediate. The body goes on an emergency full alert and prepares for physical activity. Because of the speed and urgency of this level of response it has been called the 'alarm reaction' and also the 'emergency response'. It may be that running away from danger will preserve our life or it could be that staying to fight will be more effective. We decide in a fraction of a second which course of action to take.

The alarm reaction evolved to prepare our ancestors for action when confronted by a wild animal or similar threat. A split-second decision had to be made on whether to stand their ground and fight or turn tail and flee as fast as possible. So another name for the alarm reaction is the 'fight or flight response'.

The alarm response is not an appropriate way to deal with long-term threats and demands. Here we need to make continual adjustments over a relatively long period of time. This involves mainly another part of the stress response called the 'resistance reaction'.

Many of the demands we face today are not necessarily directly life-threatening (life or death situations) but nevertheless pose threats and challenges to our personal security and wellbeing. These demands are usually emotional rather than physical in nature. Some arise unexpectedly and suddenly and last only a short time, while others persist for a long period – gnawing away day after day, week after week and even year after year. These long-term demands may include maintaining and protecting our own and our family's wellbeing and relationships, finding and keeping a job or earning a living and striving for promotion. Dealing with these situations is often distressful since it can involve struggling to establish control or fearing that control might be lost and, as a result, the safety and wellbeing of self and family is threatened.

How then is it decided which part of the stress response is activated so that the body can deal appropriately with the situation it faces?

Activation of the appropriate part of the stress response is the result of our assessment of the situation and how we think we can deal with it. This interpretation process then sets into motion a physiological reaction by the body to produce the right type of stress response. It is important to distinguish here between situations that are sudden, life-threatening ones, such as jumping clear of a car, and those which pose no actual physical threat to our life, such as being interviewed for promotion at work. For sudden, life-threatening situations there is an immediate and total activation of all parts of the stress response. However, for situations which are more psychological or emotional in nature, the stress response is activated to an appropriate degree to enable us to deal effectively with the demands we face.

Another point to remember is that any expression of the stress response is based on either the alarm (fight or flight) response or the resistance response, or both. For example, the alarm response is usually triggered just enough to allow us to deal with immediate and short-acting demands which are not life-threatening, so we may experience a little aggression or a little fear. However, sometimes we may feel so emotionally threatened by a situation (whether or not it is warranted) that the alarm response is activated to such a level that we become quite aggressive – we decide to 'fight' mentally and our body is prepared for fighting. This is one way of coping with the situation, though responding in this way may not necessarily be desirable or appropriate for our health.

On the other hand we may feel that the demand is too much for us to handle so we become scared – we mentally 'run away' from the situation while at the same time our body is geared biologically for flight.

Emotions, for example fear or anger, play a major part in our interpretation and assessment of the situations we face and hence the degree and pattern of activation of our stress response.

We can interpret a situation in three ways:

- 'I can cope with this situation' – perceived coping ability outweighs perceived demands.
- 'I am not sure whether I can cope with this situation' – doubt about perceived ability to cope with perceived demands.
- 'I cannot cope with this situation' – perceived demands outweigh perceived coping ability.

If we feel that we can handle the situation, the stress response is activated within the normal zone of the stress balance and we do not feel stressed. If we are uncertain about coping or if we feel unable to cope with a demand, the stress response will be activated beyond its normal zone giving rise to varying degrees of distress and accompanying mental 'fight or flight' or 'resistance' reactions. When we feel confident that we can deal with a demand, the stress response goes into the eustress zone. In this case, we often look forward to the challenge that a situation presents and as a result we experience eustress.

The differences in the extent of activation of the stress response within or beyond the normal zone of the stress balance depend on how you view or interpret situations around you and on how you feel about those situations. This means that stress is not in the environment but is a *state within you*. The way in which you transact with the environment determines how much and what type of stress you create for yourself.

Our interpretation of the nature of the demand and how well we feel able to cope with it depends on our experience of past events, our beliefs, attitudes, expectations and needs. These in turn depend on our genetic inheritance, personality, education, upbringing, age, sex and general state of health (Figure 6).

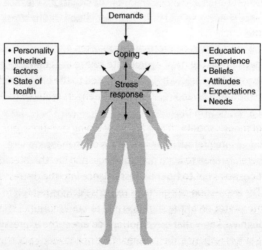

Figure 6 Factors affecting coping ability.

The appropriate response is ultimately achieved by altering the activity of the body organs to prepare the body for action. It is the job of particular chemical messengers in the body to alter organ activity. Different messengers produce different effects; for instance, one particular messenger speeds up the heart beat, while another messenger may effect a decrease in the heart rate.

The type and number of messengers required for a particular task is decided by the brain after it has received information from the senses about the nature of the demand:

- 'Is it life threatening?'
- 'Does it need to be dealt with immediately or can it wait?'
  The brain also assesses how we feel about the situation:
- 'Can I face up to it?'
- 'Am I in control of the situation?'
- 'I am angry about this.'
- 'I am concerned about this.'

The brain also recalls information from its memory store about what was learned in previous encounters.

- 'What did I do in this situation before?'
- 'This is a new experience; I'll have to tread carefully with this one.'

All these pieces of information are taken into consideration for a decision on the most appropriate course of action. Once a decision has been reached, it is transmitted to the brain, which sets in motion the various chemical messengers required to bring about a response in the body.

In today's society, in non life-threatening situations, our emotional interpretation of the event is often inappropriate. We therefore need to learn how to handle non life-threatening situations so as not to tip the stress balance into the distress zone.

The expression of our stress response can be related to our interpretation of the situation and to our emotional state. Although we know that our emotions do affect the expression of the stress response, the present state of knowledge of this link is limited.

The brain works out the most appropriate pattern of body activity to deal with the demand, and then sets into motion a sequence of events leading to the release of the appropriate cocktail of neurotransmitters and hormones to achieve this response.

The stress response is largely brought about by the action of the hormones noradrenaline, adrenaline and cortisol.

The expression of the stress response, or the way in which we deal with stress, has its roots in fight, flight or resistance.

Both noradrenaline and adrenaline are needed for fighting and fleeing. However, it is the emotion involved which determines the predominance of either noradrenaline or adrenaline, and thus the action appropriate for either running or fighting. This has given rise to a great deal of confusion over the difference between noradrenaline and adrenaline. Most people say, 'I can feel the adrenaline flowing' when they are stimulated and excited. In fact, it is noradrenaline, not adrenaline, which is associated with arousal and gives rise to feelings of excitement and drive as well as physical strength. For this reason noradrenaline has been named the 'kick' or high performance hormone which in large amounts stimulates special areas in the brain that produce a feeling of pleasure. In contrast, the feelings and sensations associated with high levels of adrenaline are not pleasant. Just think how you felt in the dentist's waiting room or waiting for a surgical operation: that was adrenaline at work, the predominant hormone released for the flight response – you probably felt like running away.

In situations where demands persist, cortisol is important in keeping up the supply of energy needed by the body for the effort required in the face of long-term demands.

Both the alarm response and resistance response operate together to assist the body in defending itself. In persistent, distressful situations we might feel like running away but cannot. Instead we must stay and cope as best we can. This can lead to lengthy periods of cortisol release. On the other hand, when faced with a non-threatening demand that will not go away, we might feel like fighting. However, the nature of the situation may not allow it, so we bottle up our feelings of irritation and anger. This can lead to an overproduction of noradrenaline. Our feelings or emotions can and do affect the activation of the stress response.

To illustrate how our emotions are related to the levels of noradrenaline, adrenaline and cortisol, let us take two situations. A man flying from Heathrow to New York has a blood sample taken just before the flight. The sample was tested for noradrenaline and adrenaline levels. At New York he hired a car to drive downtown. Another blood sample was taken before he drove off and was again tested for noradrenaline and adrenaline levels.

From these samples, the levels of noradrenaline and adrenaline can be related to the way the man was feeling at the time. Where he was not in control of the situation – a passenger on the plane – his emotions produced the relative levels of adrenaline (high) and noradrenaline (low). Having reached his destination and probably feeling relieved to be on the ground, he got into his car, drove off and felt in control of the driving situation. Once again, his emotions were reflected in the levels of noradrenaline (high) and adrenaline (low). So the level of chemicals associated with the stress response is very much determined by our emotions.

Let us take another example. Blood samples were taken from two experienced male motor rally drivers before each attempted a rally circuit and again when they had finished. The blood samples were analysed for levels of noradrenaline, adrenaline and cortisol.

Rally driving is not a race against other competitors but against time. At the end of the race, each driver will have judged how well he has performed and whether he feels he has mastered the course. The winner's blood chemistry should indicate that he felt he had mastered the circuit and performed well, so his noradrenaline levels should be higher than those of the loser. Also the winner's adrenaline and cortisol levels should be lower than those of the loser, who would be likely to feel he had not mastered the circuit and therefore did not expect to win. It is interesting to learn that the noradrenaline levels were higher at the end of the race for both drivers, reflecting the increased alertness and physical effort required for the race.

The stress response allows us to produce extremes of human performance: speed, strength and stamina. There are numerous stories describing tremendous feats of power during activation of the alarm reaction. A woman achieved the strength to lift a car releasing her trapped child. A man racing for cover during an air raid did not realize that he scaled a ten-foot wall in his dash for safety. If there had not been an emergency, neither the man nor the woman would have had the physical strength to perform these feats.

Athletes and sportsmen use the fight response to 'psych' themselves up before races and events. Observe Olympic weightlifters. Notice how they pace up and down preparing to attack the weights as though it were a sabre-toothed tiger that they are about to take on in battle. Look at the aggression and hostility in their faces and behaviour. Ready for action, they grasp the bar, 'attack', and lift.

Athletes often drive themselves to the limits of human performance. To achieve this, they must reduce the pain that arises during intense muscle activity. When they continue to perform even though they should really stop, a group of chemicals called endorphins are released in the brain to suppress the pain associated with the body's efforts. Joggers and long-distance runners owe their sustained activity to endorphins which produce a euphoric feeling. This may be one reason why joggers say they feel so good after a run when in fact they often look terrible! Being able to pass through the pain barrier is essential for survival if we are in a life or death situation and need to continue our effort until we are safe.

Chemical messenger league table

Appraisal of situation	Dominant part of stress reponse	Chemical messenger(s) order of dominance
'I can cope' 'I am in control' 'I have mastered this'	Alarm 'Fight' aspect	1 **Noradrenaline** 2 Adrenaline
'This is too demanding' 'Can I cope?'	Alarm 'Flight' aspect leading to resistance	1 **Adrenaline** 2 Cortisol
'I fear failure' 'I feel helpless' 'I am not in control' 'I have failed'	Resistance	1 **Cortisol** 2 Adrenaline 3 Noradrenaline

2

stress, health and performance

Most signs of stress can be explained by the actions of the stress response in the body. The stress hormones – adrenaline, noradrenaline and cortisol are mostly responsible for the manifestation of signs, when the stress response is over-activated and the stress balance tips out of the normal zone.

A questionnaire will help you identify your key signs and symptoms arising from the activity of your stress response. This will help you to monitor your reaction to the demands and pressures you encounter. You will be able to identify these from self-assessment questionnaires in Chapter 3.

Monitoring your signs and symptoms can provide you with a guide to show how effective your stress management techniques are for dealing with stress, since the fewer signs and symptoms you have, the more effective you are at dealing with your stressors and hence managing the activity of your stress response.

Assessing your signs and symptoms

Before we describe the physical, mental and behavioural signs and symptoms of distress, you can assess some of your own signs and symptoms by completing the questionnaire below. For this questionnaire, we have selected some of the more usually manifested signs and symptoms.

Signs and Symptoms

Tick the most appropriate box

During the last month have you:	(a) Almost never	(b) Sometimes	(c) Most of the time	(d) Almost all the time
1 been easily irritated by people or trivial events?	❑	❑	❑	❑
2 felt impatient?	❑	❑	❑	❑
3 felt unable to cope?	❑	❑	❑	❑
4 felt a failure?	❑	❑	❑	❑
5 found it difficult to make decisions?	❑	❑	❑	❑
6 lost interest in other people?	❑	❑	❑	❑
7 felt you had no one to confide in or to talk to about your problems?	❑	❑	❑	❑
8 found it difficult to concentrate?	❑	❑	❑	❑

Tick the most appropriate box

During the last month have you:	(a) Almost never	(b) Sometimes	(c) Most of the time	(d) Almost all the time
9 failed to finish tasks/jobs before moving on to the next, leaving jobs incomplete?	❑	❑	❑	❑
10 felt neglected in any way?	❑	❑	❑	❑
11 tried to do too many things at once?	❑	❑	❑	❑
12 felt anxious or depressed?	❑	❑	❑	❑
13 been uncharacteristically aggressive?	❑	❑	❑	❑
14 felt bored?	❑	❑	❑	❑
15 changed your patterns of drinking, smoking or eating?	❑	❑	❑	❑
16 changed your level of sexual activity?	❑	❑	❑	❑
17 cried or had the desire to cry?	❑	❑	❑	❑
18 felt tired most of the time?	❑	❑	❑	❑

(*contd.*)

Tick the most appropriate box

During the last month have you:	(a) Almost never	(b) Sometimes	(c) Most of the time	(d) Almost all the time
19 suffered from any of the following more frequently – back and neck pain, headaches, muscular aches and pains, muscular spasms and cramps, constipation, diarrhoea, loss of appetite, heartburn, indigestion and nausea?	❑	❑	❑	❑
20 Do two or more of the following apply to you – bite your nails, clench your fists, drum your fingers, grind your teeth, hunch your shoulders, tap your feet, have trouble falling or staying asleep?	❑	❑	❑	❑
Total				

Scoring

Questions 1, 5, 7, 8, 14, 16, 17 and 18
   Score (d) 6 (c) 4 (b) 2 (a) 0
Questions 2, 6, 9, 10, 11, 15, 19 and 20
   Score (d) 3 (c) 2 (b) 1 (a) 0
Questions 3, 4, 12 and 13
   Score (d) 30 (c) 20 (b) 10 (a) 0

Evaluation

If your score is over 30, then you are most likely to be suffering from distress. The higher you score towards the maximum of 192 the more distress you are suffering. Scores of over 60 are a cause for concern and indicate that you should discuss your lifestyle with your doctor.

Select the three highest scoring items. This will help remind you what to look for as you monitor your body's physical activity and your behaviour.

The brief questionnaire you have just completed does not address all the signs and symptoms, so we give a more comprehensive list below. Study the list so you are aware of the range of the signs and symptoms of distress.

Signs of distress

Physical

- Awareness of heart beating, palpitations
- Breathlessness, lump in the throat, rapid shallow breathing
- Dry mouth, 'butterflies' in stomach, indigestion, nausea
- Diarrhoea, constipation, flatulence
- General muscle tenseness particularly of the jaws, grinding of teeth
- Clenched fists, hunched shoulders, general muscle aches and pains, cramps

- Restlessness, hyperactivity, nail biting, finger drumming, foot tapping, hands shaking
- Tiredness, fatigue, lethargy, exhaustion, sleep difficulties, feeling faint, headaches, frequent illnesses such as colds
- Sweatiness especially palms and upper lip, hot flushed feeling
- Cold hands and feet
- Frequent desire to urinate
- Overeating, loss of appetite, increased cigarette smoking
- Increased alcohol consumption, loss of interest in sex.

Mental

- Distress, worry, upset, tearfulness, feeling deflated, feelings of helplessness and hopelessness, hysteria, seeming withdrawn, feeling unable to cope, anxiety, depression
- Impatience, being easily irritated and aggravated, feeling angry, hostile, aggressive
- Frustration, boredom, inadequacy, guilt, rejection, neglect, insecurity, vulnerability
- Loss of interest in self-appearance, health, diet, sex; low self-esteem, loss of interest in others
- Polyphasic (doing too many things at once), rushed
- Failing to finish tasks before moving on to the next
- Difficulty in thinking clearly, concentrating and making decisions, forgetfulness, lack of creativity, irrationality; procrastination, difficulty in starting to do things
- Being prone to make mistakes and having accidents
- Having so much to do and not knowing where to start so ending up doing nothing or going from task to task and not completing anything
- Being hypercritical, inflexible, unreasonable, over-reactive, non-productive, poor efficiency.

You should note that this list is not exhaustive and some of the mental signs could be regarded as physical signs and vice versa.

Signs of eustress

Clearly, an absence of the signs and symptoms of distress indicates that you are not suffering the bad effects of stress. The signs of eustress paint a picture of how you might feel when you are harnessing the positive aspects of the stress response. You might feel and appear:

- euphoric, stimulated, thrilled, excited
- helpful, understanding, sociable, friendly, loving, happy
- calm, controlled, confident
- creative, effective, efficient
- clear and rational in thought, decisive
- industrious, lively, productive, jolly, often smiling.

The stress response and signs of stress

We have described how the stress response is mediated via different chemicals, notably noradrenaline, adrenaline and cortisol, so that different body actions can take place. It is possible to identify those signs in the body and mind which are produced by the action of noradrenaline, adrenaline or cortisol.

Noradrenaline

Noradrenaline is associated with aggression and fighting behaviour as shown by changes in facial muscle tenseness and drawing back of lips to show the teeth which are clenched together. The back and shoulder muscles tense (hunched shoulders) and the fists clench. Hairs stand more erect; this is seen as 'goose pimples' since humans have relatively little body hair compared to other animals. All this action is to make us look more threatening and hostile. Also, the skin blood vessels constrict, and the palms of the hands, the feet and the upper lip become sweaty. The pupil of the eye dilates, mental alertness increases, thinking and decision-making become quicker and performance improves.

Noradrenaline produces a feeling of pleasantness and excitement in the absence of irritation, anger and hostility.

Adrenaline

Adrenaline on the other hand is more orientated toward preparing the body for a quick getaway. Heart action increases and can be felt as a pounding in the chest. This is sometimes erratic and described as heart palpitations. Blood supply to the vital organs and skeletal muscles increases so it is necessary for noradrenaline to reduce the supply to the non-vital organs such as the gut and skin. This, together with a reduction in activity of the gut, gives the feeling of 'butterflies' and knots in the stomach. A 'cold sweat' is experienced when sweat is secreted onto the surface of a cold skin.

Feelings of uncertainty, worry, insecurity and anxiety are examples of the results of adrenaline activity.

Cortisol

Outward physical signs that cortisol is at work are difficult to see although frequent colds, allergies or asthma could be indicators. However, the mental signs are clear enough: feelings of failure, helplessness, hopelessness, chronic anxiety, depression.

It is also important that you can identify the signs of stress in others: your family, friends and work colleagues.

Being alert to the signs of distress in others will help you to reduce relationship problems and maintain a creative and productive office and organization.

At work it would be foolish to pile more tasks onto your colleague who is rushing around trying to do too many things at once and becoming impatient, easily irritated at trivial things and snappy with workmates. Or to ignore an overloaded colleague who has problems at home and perhaps withdraws, becomes uncharacteristically quiet and looks depressed. Watch out also for the colleague who becomes frustrated and bored because there is too little to do and who feels their abilities and talents are not being adequately used.

Not all the signs are exclusively signs of stress

Care must be taken in interpreting the signs of stress since many can be due to other factors. For instance, cold hands can be due to winter weather! A low external temperature is a physical stressor because it activates the body's stress response, within the normal zone, so that a normal body temperature can be maintained. Unless the temperatures are extreme and potentially life-threatening, most people would not say they felt 'stressed' because of them. So a person might have cold hands but not feel emotionally stressed at the time. Furthermore, some diseases of the circulation can lead to poor blood flow in the hands, resulting in coldness.

Signs such as back and neck pain, headaches, muscular aches and pains, spasm and cramps, constipation, diarrhoea, indigestion and nausea can all arise for reasons other than stress. The symptoms of some diseases and conditions, for example Irritable Bowel Syndrome, are those we also see attributed to stress. It is when we find a number of these signs occurring together, in the absence of diagnosed health problems, that we can often attribute them to stress.

Hidden signs

It is impossible for us to see blood glucose and fat levels changing, more red cells pouring into the bloodstream, blood clotting more easily or wound-healing processes being stimulated when the stress response is at work. These signs are hidden from our eyes but not from the scientist who, with an array of highly sophisticated instruments, can spot and measure the internal actions of the stress response.

Unfortunately many of the hidden signs outwardly rear their ugly heads only when it is too late. Their continued or frequent action can lead to ill health and death and only then can they be seen! Take heed of outward physical and mental signs of stress and take preventive action before it is too late!

Some distress-related disorders and diseases

Cardiovascular system

Coronary heart disease (angina and heart attacks)
Hypertension (high blood pressure)
Strokes
Migraine

Digestive system

Indigestion
Nausea
Heartburn
Stomach and duodenal ulcers
Ulcerative colitis
Irritable bowel syndrome
Diarrhoea
Constipation
Flatulence

Muscles and joints

Headaches
Cramps
Muscle spasm
Back pain
Neck pain

Other

Diabetes
Cancers
Rheumatoid arthritis
Allergies
Asthma
Common cold and flu
Sexual disorders – reduced sex drive, premature ejaculation, failure to reach orgasm, infertility
Skin disorders
Sleep disorders

Behavioural

Overeating – obesity
Loss of appetite – anorexia
Increased cigarette smoking
Increased caffeine intake
Increased alcohol consumption
Drug abuse

Emotional

Anxiety, including fears, phobias and obsessions
Depression

Homo sapiens has existed for around 40,000 years in essentially the same biological form as we are today. The urbanized, industrialized, high technology era is a very recent phenomenon in this evolutionary period but has presented the greatest amount of environmental change in a relatively short time. We still have the same biological mechanism – the stress response – to deal with a very different environment.

Today we are bombarded with a continuous stream of emotional threats and challenges and if our beliefs lead us regularly to perceive these as stressors, real or imaginary, then we face the consequences of ill health and death as a result of over-using our stress response.

A number of research studies have shown how blood cholesterol levels rise during periods of stress. In one such experiment, blood cholesterol was measured in two groups of accountants throughout a period of about six months. During this time, the accountants were asked to keep a record of their lifestyle (diet, exercise and so on) and also how much pressure and stress they experienced. Accountants were chosen for the experiment because they work to deadlines. In fact, one group were tax accountants who had one deadline to meet in April while the others were corporate accountants who had deadlines in January and April. Figure 7 shows that, for both groups, there is a peak in blood cholesterol levels coinciding with the deadlines: one for the tax accountants and two for the corporate accountants. Almost all the accountants reported feeling pressured around the time of the deadline but there was no reported significant change in diet or exercise.

When the level of fat in the blood increases, the blood becomes thicker and more viscous. This also occurs when more red cells are pumped into the circulation from the spleen during the stress response. The heart must work harder to circulate thicker blood, therefore myocardial oxygen consumption increases. Another problem with thicker blood is that red blood cells can form a 'sludge' which may block small blood vessels. Sludging in the very small blood vessels of the heart and brain can lead to a heart attack or stroke respectively.

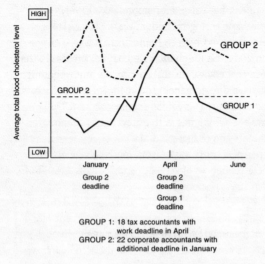

GROUP 1: 18 tax accountants with
work deadline in April
GROUP 2: 22 corporate accountants with
additional deadline in January

adapted from: Friedman & Rosenman Circ. 17.852–861 1958

Figure 7 Average blood cholesterol level in accountants as they face deadlines.

Stress and performance

Too little stimulation, too few demands and challenges
can lead to boredom, frustration and a feeling that we are not
using our abilities to the full. This situation will tip the stress
balance into the distress zone and result in poor performance
in whatever we do. Similarly, excessive demands can be
very distressful, for example, work overload, extreme time
pressure, inescapable demands imposed by others, and too
many stressful life events. Such demands can make us feel
that control is slipping away, we start doubting our ability
to cope and consequently our performance suffers. This is
particularly so where the tasks are complicated, unusual or
unfamiliar. On the other hand, where we perceive demands
and challenges as well within our capabilities and we feel
confident in handling the task, then performance improves

and reaches a peak. However, even those who usually cope well will inevitably suffer some reduction of performance when they are under extreme pressure and dealing with excessive demands. Too much effort and trying too hard often fails to achieve the desired result. Working flat out under high pressure (that is, many demands) to get things done is not always the right strategy, as can be seen in Figure 8. This way of working may achieve goals in the short term, but working at high pressure over a long period will inevitably take its toll on the performance, productivity, relationships and health of most people.

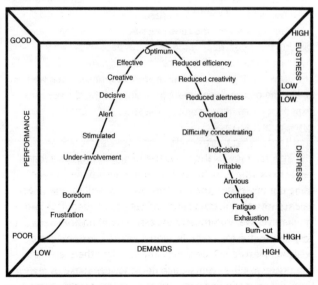

Figure 8 Stress and performance.

Working in this way is like running a car without stopping to service it. As long as the tank is filled with petrol, the engine will keep running, but what happens when the tyres lose air and the spark plugs are not changed? Performance drops. Eventually, if the car continues to be driven without any attention, it will break down.

Some people can successfully concentrate a high workload into a short period and achieve effective results but they know when to stop for a break. They take the necessary time to relax and recharge their batteries.

Maximum performance is achieved on the top part of the upward slope of the performance curve where we feel stimulated, alert, are better at making decisions, are more creative and effective in achieving results.

Peak performance is reached when we are dealing with just the right number and type of demands and challenges and we feel confident and well able to handle them.

However, if demands and pressures continue to increase beyond this point, our coping resources become steadily overtaxed and our performance starts to decline. We hit the downward slope of the curve. If this continues, then we could find ourselves on the slippery slope of the distress zone: experiencing anxiety, fatigue, exhaustion and mental breakdown, often referred to as 'burn-out'.

Looking back at the actions of the stress response and the effects of noradrenaline and adrenaline, it is clear to see how stress affects performance. Noradrenaline increases alertness, improves concentration, mental ability, learning and decision-making and it makes us feel good. Adrenaline has none of these benefits and makes us feel awful. It can make us forget things more easily, reduce concentration and decision-making ability.

Being in the eustress zone means having a predominance of noradrenaline activity. But do not be alarmed after having read about how noradrenaline can lead to ill health and death! Being in the eustress zone means activating the stress response by just the right amount so that you feel confident in dealing with your demands and challenges. The amount of noradrenaline released in the body to achieve this is not harmful. It is only when excessive amounts of noradrenaline are released that harm may arise. This can occur when too much eustress is experienced. Too many eustressful demands can overtax the body in a similar way to many distressful demands. You can have too much of a good thing!

sources
of stress

Any object, event or situation in the environment that triggers activation of our stress response is termed a "stressor".

Our beliefs and attitudes establish our perceptions and hence our personal triggers. Some individuals display Type A Behaviour. They see situations as threatening or challenging, when in fact no real threat exists. In so doing, they generate unnecessary stress for themselves. Such stress can be avoided by learning to modify their behaviour.

On the other hand, some events or situations during our lives will certainly be stressful. An appreciation that life events are unavoidable can raise awareness of the need to take stock of coping resources and learn more about stress management techniques.

Questionnaires in this chapter can help you identify significant stressors in your life that arise from your behaviour, your personal circumstances and from your work environment. Identifying these stressors will help you decide on more effective ways of learning to manage your stress.

The nature of the demands

We are most likely to experience stress in our relationships with others, particularly at work and at home.

Much of this stress is associated with threats and challenges to our self-esteem and self-image, the security and stability of our jobs and family relationships.

However, there are some physical stressors that are clearly life-threatening and we would all see them as such. We see that we are in danger with little time to plan our action, so our alarm response is quickly summoned. Most of us also treat novel and unusual situations as stressors, since we have no past experience in dealing with them. For these and other stressors, the amount and type of stress experienced and the activity level of the stress response depends on how we perceive the nature of the demand or threat. How important is it to us, how long does it last, how often does it occur and how clear are we about what is happening? To illustrate the nature of the demands, we can use the example of being held up in heavy traffic.

Importance of the stressor

Some people do not mind being held up in heavy, slow-moving traffic since losing some time is of no importance to them. On the other hand others 'tear their hair out' because the delay will make them late for an important meeting. They may become angry and hostile towards other drivers, especially those jumping the queue. The point is that the importance of the stressor to you will determine the degree to which your stress response is activated.

Duration of the stressor

Being held up in a traffic jam for a few minutes may cause some irritation in a driver who is late for a meeting but if the traffic jam persists, he may 'blow a fuse'. How long each stressor lasts will affect your stress balance and the extent to which your stress response is activated.

Intensity of the stressor

Our delayed driver will probably react less strongly to a queue of ten cars ahead than he would to a queue of 100 cars stretching into the distance.

Frequency of the stressor

Getting out of one traffic jam only to find himself in another can keep our driver's fuse smouldering. He may meet unexpected traffic hold-ups every day while commuting: a car broken down, an accident or a lorry shedding its load. How often stressors occur will determine where your stress balance lies and to what extent your stress response is activated.

Uncertainty about the stressor

As our delayed driver approaches the traffic jam he may immediately treat it as a stressor because he is uncertain how long he will be delayed. 'How far does this hold-up go on for?' he mutters to himself as he views the line of traffic disappearing round the next bend. 'What will happen if I'm late for my meeting?' For many of us, worrying about what is *likely* to happen is a major source of distress.

Type A Behaviour

In the mid 1950s, two American cardiologists investigated the possible role of emotional stress in bringing on a heart attack. They asked several hundred industrialists and 100 doctors treating coronary patients, 'What do you think caused the heart attack of a friend or patient?' The majority said stress. The pressure to meet deadlines and excessive competition were singled out as the main culprits. Fascinated by the fact that emotional stress might play a role in coronary heart disease, these two cardiologists started to look at their own patients in a different way. As well as taking blood pressure and assessing cholesterol levels, they looked for signs of emotional stress. It soon emerged that many of their coronary patients behaved in a similar way. Body movements and speech characteristics, as well as what the patients said during consultations, painted the same picture of individuals who were rushed, impatient, excessively competitive, ambitious and easily irritated. These early observations of what became known as Type A Behaviour formed the basis of much research investigating the link between emotional stress and heart disease.

So what exactly is Type A Behaviour? We described earlier how much of the way in which we interpret situations depends on our beliefs, attitudes and expectations.

Type A individuals have beliefs, attitudes and expectations that engage them in a constant struggle to gain control over their environment.

Type A people battle vigorously to achieve and maintain control, and when they sense this is being challenged or threatened, they respond by behaving in a Type A manner. Each time Type As perceive such emotional threats and challenges, they *automatically* trigger their stress response. But there is no *real* threat or challenge to their life. As a result, they generate much unnecessary stress for themselves which keeps them frequently outside the normal zone of the stress balance and in the distress zone. Traffic jams, queues at the supermarket and bank, and finding the toothpaste squeezed from the middle of the tube are examples of situations that Type As find threatening. So in response to these situations, their heart rate accelerates and pounds, their blood clots more easily and cholesterol levels rise – all for no purpose. With his body prepared for physical action by activation of the stress response, the Type A individual can only sit and fume in his car. He cannot get out and run up and down the traffic lanes or abandon his car and run away; nor can he engage in a fight with other motorists.

You need to identify Type A Behaviour in yourself so that you can take steps to reduce and modify it. This is possible because Type A Behaviour is primarily a learned way of interacting with the environment. Type A Behaviour is chiefly identified by a constant sense of time urgency and easily aroused irritation and aggravation. It is observed in an individual who tries to do more and more in less and less time, thinks about or does two or more things simultaneously, and frequently becomes angry in response to trivial happenings.

Type As might be described as agitated, hard-driving, hasty, hostile, hurried, impatient and irritable. They are often poor listeners, rushed, over-competitive and over-ambitious. People who have very few of these characteristics are described as Type B. They are calm, content, controlled, easy-going, good listeners, not easily irritated, patient and unhurried. Type A and Type B behaviour can be assessed objectively.

The questionnaire below will provide a measure of this. For each question tick the box that best represents your behaviour.

Type A Behaviour

For each question, tick the box that best represents your behaviour.

	Never	Almost never	Sometimes	Usually	Almost always	Always
Are you late for appointments?	❑	❑	❑	❑	❑	❑
Are you competitive in the games you play at home or at work?	❑	❑	❑	❑	❑	❑
In conversations, do you anticipate what others are going to say (head nod, interrupt, finish sentences for them)?	❑	❑	❑	❑	❑	❑
Do you have to do things in a hurry?	❑	❑	❑	❑	❑	❑
Do you get impatient in queues or traffic jams?	❑	❑	❑	❑	❑	❑
Do you try to do several things at once and think about what you are about to do next?	❑	❑	❑	❑	❑	❑

	Never	Almost never	Sometimes	Usually	Almost always	Always
Do you feel you do most things quickly (eating, walking, talking, driving)?	❑	❑	❑	❑	❑	❑
Do you get easily irritated over trivia?	❑	❑	❑	❑	❑	❑
If you make a mistake, do you get angry with yourself?	❑	❑	❑	❑	❑	❑
Do you find fault with and criticize other people?	❑	❑	❑	❑	❑	❑
Total						

Scoring

5 = Always
4 = Almost always
3 = Usually
2 = Sometimes
1 = Almost never
0 = Never

Total your scores and multiply by 2.

Evaluation

Type B	0–39	You are slightly and/or rarely impatient and aggravated. You create hardly any unnecessary stress for yourself and your health is probably unaffected.

Mild Type A	40–59	You are fairly and/or occasionally impatient and aggravated. You create some unnecessary stress for yourself and this may affect your health.
Moderate Type A	60–79	You are very and/or often impatient and aggravated. You generate much unnecessary stress for yourself and this may affect your health.
Extreme Type A	80–100	You are extremely and/or usually impatient and aggravated. You generate too much unnecessary stress for yourself and this may affect your health.

You should note that this is a self-assessment of your Type A Behaviour. It is only as accurate as you are honest in your answers. Furthermore, Type As are often blind to their own behaviour, for example, doing things fast. Type As may not think they are as fast as they actually are.

The questionnaire is based on some common Type A characteristics, many of which are simple to detect, while others are subtle and not so obviously related to time urgency and easily aroused anger and hostility. If a person possesses a large number of Type A characteristics and displays these frequently and excessively, then he is considered to be an extreme Type A. On a scale of 0–100, the spectrum of Type A Behaviour ranges from mild (score 40–59 per cent) and moderate (score 60–79 per cent) to severe (score 80–100 per cent), with Type B individuals described as having very few Type A characteristics (score of 39 per cent or less). Using a similar questionnaire, we have surveyed over 5,000 people and found that only 10 per cent were Type B, 80 per cent mild to moderate Type A, and 10 per cent extreme Type A.

Identifying Type A Behaviour

To help you identify Type A Behaviour, we will describe some typical and some extreme examples.

In an attempt to gain control, Type As become 'hurry sick'; they adopt two strategies with which to save time to get more and more done in less and less time. Firstly, they practise 'speedup' – doing things fast to save time. So they eat fast, walk fast, drive fast and talk fast. Some Type As take 'speedup' to extremes. Type A men have admitted to shaving with two electric razors at once, to save time! On hearing this, a woman reporter admitted to us that she blow-dries her hair with two hairdryers at the same time. But incredible though these actions may seem to Type Bs, and also to many Type As for that matter, they are insignificant when compared to the man who liquidizes all his meals so he can drink them to save time!

Not content with the amount of time saved by 'speedup', Type As turn to 'polyphasing' – doing two or more things at the same time. So they clean their teeth or shave while taking a shower, or continue writing a document while engaged in a telephone conversation on a completely different subject. As they drive to work, Type As shave, apply make-up, eat breakfast or read the morning paper. Extreme Type As regard it as a challenge to see how many different things they can do at the same time. We heard of a businessman in San Francisco who installed a hinged desktop in his toilet so that he could continue working while attending to the call of nature.

Wasting time in queues is something Type As cannot tolerate. They will seek ways in which to beat, jump or avoid queuing at the bank, post office, shops, garage, traffic lights and so on. Take the supermarket situation and an extreme

Type A shopper coming up to the checkouts. While nobody would choose to join the longest queue, our extreme Type A shopper will make several decisions before selecting a queue. First, Type As count the number of people in the queue then multiply this by the number of items in each basket and trolley. Many of us may well do this, but Type As will go further. They assess the efficiency of the checkout operator before making their choice of which queue to join. A decision is made and the 'fastest' queue joined. Now, instead of simply queuing, Type As take other people as markers in other queues to see if they have made the right choice. Noradrenaline levels start to rise when our Type A realizes that the markers are making better progress – 'Why do I always choose the wrong queue?', our Type A curses. Noradrenaline levels then hit the roof when the person in front of their queue holds them up by paying by credit card or cheque, and sky-high levels are reached when they get to the checkout and the till roll runs out. Our Type A finally leaves the store angry at himself and quick to vent this anger on others. Learning from this situation, Type As have adopted several strategies to beat the supermarket queue. One Type A proudly described how he took six trolleys and put five items in each and went through the express checkout six times!

The supermarket battleground may give rise to a few confrontations with other shoppers, but impatience in the driving situation exposes the ugly side of extreme Type A Behaviour. The typical Type A driver will always strive to drive as fast as possible, jump the red light and make Grand Prix starts just as the lights turn green. They relentlessly and obsessively drive close to the car in front and overtake at any possible, or even near-impossible, opportunity. They will compulsively switch lanes in traffic jams and take alternative routes in an attempt to avoid an apparent hold-up, often not knowing exactly where they are heading!

One extreme Type A recalled how he fought a constant stress battle always to avoid any lane which might be bottled up.

'If I see a slow-moving car or lorry I'm out of its way before I'm anywhere near to it,' he exclaimed. In fact, he admitted that his driving behaviour in this respect was so successful that he usually arrived early for his appointments and had to sit in his car and wait!

Type As find it difficult to believe that their way of behaving is counter-productive. Type Bs give themselves more time and space to be creative and are more effective in the long run, often advancing their careers!

Contrary to popular belief, Type Bs are also ambitious and competitive people, but they go about things in a different way; they have a more laid-back, rational attitude.

As a result, they achieve their goals without suffering ill health. They usually have more fulfilling family relationships and a good social life.

Frequently, Type As find it difficult to relax and switch off from work. They are the people who come back from the Costa del Sol with three white lines across their forehead or who telephone the office every day or pack business work in their suitcase. Often they feel obliged to take work home and are only happy if their briefcases are bulging at the seams!

Type As will often say, 'I thrive on stress'. In fact, what they are saying is, 'I am addicted to noradrenaline'. This addiction produces a feeling of confidence and elation and often leads Type As to seek out challenging situations to keep their noradrenaline levels high.

Are you addicted to noradrenaline?

Signs of noradrenaline addiction:

- Mind frequently racing
- Difficulty in getting to sleep
- Smoking too much
- Drinking too much caffeine
- Hyperactive.

Excessive, frequent and prolonged release of noradrenaline is thought to increase the risk of heart disease, high blood pressure, migraine and ulcers. Type As usually over-react to challenges and threats and, faced with a demanding situation, release much noradrenaline.

Unfortunately, self-induced stress in Type As often distorts their perception and they fail to recognize what is happening to them. However, not all Type As succumb to the ill effects of stress. It has been suggested that a personality factor described as 'hardiness' (stress resistance) interacts with Type A Behaviour to minimize its risk to health. Hardy people look upon situations as challenges rather than threats. They have commitment to what they do and feel confident about gaining control. They turn stressful life events into possibilities or opportunities for personal growth and benefit. More research is needed in this area to clarify the involvement of hardiness with stress and health.

The stress generated by Type A Behaviour is avoidable by modifying beliefs, attitudes and habits.

Life events

Some stressors are unavoidable and will affect most of us at some time during our lives. These are often referred to as 'life events' and are crises that must be faced, for example, illness and injury to yourself, family and friends, and bereavement. Other crises may occur, such as marital disharmony, problems with children, financial difficulties and work problems. There are also events that require some adjustment on our part, such as moving to a new house, changing jobs, children starting school. Our stress response is activated to help us deal with these changes, events and crises.

Research has shown that if we experience too many life events during a short period, our adaptive and coping resources may be overtaxed and this can lead to ill health.

Complete the questionnaire below to assess whether your life events are putting you at a higher risk of ill health.

Life events questionnaire

	TICK	SCORE		TICK	SCORE
Death of a partner	☐	___	Child leaves home	☐	___
Divorce	☐	___	Trouble with in-laws	☐	___
Separation from partner	☐	___	Outstanding personal achievement	☐	___
Jail sentence	☐	___	Partner begins or stops work	☐	___
Death of a close family member	☐	___	Child begins or ends school	☐	___
Injury or illness to yourself	☐	___	Change in living conditions	☐	___
Marriage – your own	☐	___	Change of personal habits	☐	___
Given the sack at work	☐	___	Trouble with boss or employer	☐	___
Reconciliation with partner	☐	___	Change in working hours and conditions	☐	___
Retirement	☐	___	Change in residence	☐	___
Ill health in member of family	☐	___	Child changes schools	☐	___
Pregnancy – your own	☐	___	Change in recreation	☐	___
Sexual problems/difficulties	☐	___	Change in church activities	☐	___
Addition of new family member	☐	___	Change in social activities	☐	___
Major business or work changes	☐	___	Take on a small mortgage or loan	☐	___
Change in your financial state	☐	___	Change in sleeping habits	☐	___
Death of a friend	☐	___	Change in number of family get-togethers	☐	___
Change to a different type of work	☐	___	Change in eating habits	☐	___
More arguments with partner	☐	___	Holiday	☐	___
Take on a large mortgage	☐	___	Christmas (coming soon)	☐	___
Mortgage or loan foreclosed	☐	___	Minor violations of the law	☐	___
Change in responsibilities at work	☐	___	TOTAL SCORE		☐

This scale is adapted from Holmes and Rahe's Life Change Index, *Journal of Psychosomatic Research*, 1967 Vol. 11.

Tick off the listed events which you have experienced during the last 12 months, then check your list against the scores for each item. Write your score in the box for each item and then add up the scores. Write your total score in the box.

Scoring

Death of partner	100	Child leaves home	29
Divorce	73	Trouble with in-laws	29
Separation from partner	65	Outstanding personal achievement	28
Jail sentence	63	Partner begins or stops work	26
Death of a close family member	63	Child begins or ends school	26
Injury or illness to yourself	53	Change in living conditions	25
Marriage – your own	50	Change of personal habits	24
Given the sack at work	47	Trouble with boss or employer	23
Reconciliation with partner	45	Change in working hours and conditions	20
Retirement	45	Change in residence	20
Ill health in member of family	44	Child changes schools	20
Pregnancy – your own	40	Change in recreation	19
Sexual problems/ difficulties	39	Change in church activities	19
Addition of new family member	39	Change in social activities	18
Major business or work changes	39	Take on a small mortgage or loan	17
Change in your financial state	38	Change in sleeping habits	16
Death of a friend	37	Change in number of family get-togethers	15
Change to a different type of work	36	Change in eating habits	15
More arguments with partner	35	Holiday	13
Take on a large mortgage	31	Christmas (coming soon)	12
Mortgage or loan foreclosed	30	Minor violations of the law	11
Change in responsibilities at work	29		

Evaluation

Your risk of illness during the next two years if you score 300 or more is 80 per cent; for a score of 150–299 it is 50 per cent; for a score of 100–149 it is 30 per cent. Less than 100 indicates no change in risk.

The life events scale was developed by researchers in the United States while undertaking a study to establish which events occurring during a person's life required the most readjustment. Forty-three life events making up the questionnaire were selected as being the most common and stressful. You will notice that some events, such as illness and bereavement, are traumatic and likely to give rise to distress whereas others, such as marriage, birth of a child or moving house, might be expected to be pleasant and enjoyable experiences. However, they all require a change in the person's life as they readjust to the new situation. Each event is given a score on a scale from 0 to 100. The scores are based on how much adjustment people felt they needed to make in order to cope with each situation, if getting married is rated at 50 points. As expected, most people rated death of a spouse at the maximum score of 100, while at the other end of the scale, Christmas was valued at 12 and minor violations of the law, 11. Subsequent research using this scale showed that those people who scored over 100 points in their previous year had an increased risk of suffering a major illness during the next two years.

Even though these types of stressor are unavoidable, our beliefs and attitudes can play a major part in how we perceive them and how much stress, if any, we experience. For example, bereavement is undoubtedly a major stressor, but our religious beliefs may reduce the stress experienced.

Family, social and work situations

We spend about a third of our life at work, a further third sleeping and the remaining third with our family and friends. Many people find that the most distress in their lives arises from relationships with others, both in the family and social setting, and at work. Look back at the life events list and you will see how many are associated with relationships, for example, marital disharmony, problems with children, problems with neighbours, problems with the boss or co-workers. Similarly, there are a number of events relating to work. Work is commonly cited as a major cause of distress and there are many reasons for this, for example:

- work overload – simply having too much to do
- time pressures and impossible deadlines to meet
- how well and to what extent you feel your skills and abilities are being used
- poorly defined or understood job role
- changes in procedures
- poor communication – not knowing what is going on and not feeling part of the organization.

Sometimes these demands may be imposed on you by others and you feel pressured and not in control. Use the 'Identifying stress at work' questionnaire below to assess your level of job satisfaction. Being dissatisfied with a particular aspect of your job may not mean you find it stressful so you should also rate your perceived stress experience for each item.

Identifying stress at work

This questionnaire is a guide to help identify stressors at work. For each aspect of your job write the stress rating to indicate how much stress you experience. Add your scores and write the total in the box.

Stress rating

0 = no stress
1 = slightly stressful
2 = moderately stressful
3 = very stressful
4 = extremely stressful

Aspects of your job	Stress rating
The physical conditions at work, e.g. ventilation, noise, lighting, heating	❑
The freedom to choose your work	❑
The freedom to get on with your work colleagues	❑
The recognition you get for good work	❑
Having more than one immediate boss	❑
Your immediate boss or bosses	❑
The amount of responsibility you are given	❑
Your rate of pay	❑
Your opportunity to use your abilities	❑
Industrial relations between management and workers in your organization	❑
Your chance of promotion	❑
The way your organization is managed	❑
The attention paid to suggestions you make	❑
The number of hours worked	❑
The amount of variety in your job	❑
The security of your employment	❑
Any other aspects	❑
Total score	▢

Evaluation

Below 21: Your job does not appear to cause you too much distress.

21 to 40: It appears that your job may be the source of some distress.

41 to 60: Your job appears to be a cause of much distress.

Above 60: Your job appears to be a major source of distress.

Carrying out this exercise will help you to focus on those aspects at work which may be sources of stress for you. This is a first step for dealing with stress at work.

Work stress can also be self-imposed, for example, setting unrealistic goals, attempting to change too much too quickly. You may need to stand back and ask yourself how your stress is arising. Are you asking too much of people who work for you? Are you creating unnecessary stress for yourself? Are you a workaholic?

It may be that you regard your stress as being derived only from work or home but usually it is from both. Stress from family arguments or financial worries can affect our work performance; our minds might not be on the job at hand and accidents or mistakes can easily occur. Feeling generally distressed will make us less able to handle the inevitable pressures and demands of our job. On the other hand, a happy home life with few major worries can help us ride through the pressures of work without distress. Similarly, a day at work full of pressure, demands and situations that lower our self-esteem can continue when we get home. Then it takes just a minor irritation to make us snap at our partner or shout at the children.

Often before we realize what is happening, we can enter into a vicious circle and things can go from bad to worse. So stress must be tackled throughout all aspects of our lives.

We should remember that family, social and work situations can be a source of much joy, love, support and stimulation.

They can provide security and self-esteem. Building on these can keep you away from the distress zone and direct you into the eustress zone.

stress management

To improve stress management effectiveness, we need to understand the principles of stress balance adjustment. This involves knowing how to alter the activity of the stress response. There are a number of processes that can achieve the right balance for more effective stress management. All such processes involve learning to balance coping ability against demands.

We have selected three examples to illustrate how to adjust the stress balance:

- learning to alter emotional and physical demands
- learning to actively relax
- learning to modify Type A Behaviour

These processes involve the employment of a range of therapies and activities that can assist the learning process, for example cognitive behavioural therapy and other talking therapies, meditation and progressive muscular relaxation.

Practising a variety of techniques will build up experience needed to tackle stress in the long term. Planning what to do in advance can reduce potential distress. This preventative approach is the essence of effective stress management.

Getting the right balance

You can assess your current coping ability by completing the following questionnaire.

Coping ability

Tick either Yes or No to each question.	Yes	No
1 Do you have supportive family/friends?	☐	☐
2 Do you have a hobby?	☐	☐
3 Do you belong to a social or activity group?	☐	☐
4 Do you practise an active relaxation technique (yoga, meditation, imagery, autogenic training, etc.) on a daily basis?	☐	☐
5 Do you exercise for at least 20 minutes three times a week?	☐	☐
6 Do you do something 'just for yourself' each week that you really enjoy?	☐	☐
7 Do you have somewhere you can go in order to be alone?	☐	☐
8 Have you attended a stress management, relaxation, time management or assertiveness training course?	☐	☐
9 Do you show Type B Behaviour?	☐	☐
10 Do you smoke?	☐	☐
11 Do you drink alcohol to relax?	☐	☐
12 Do you take sleeping pills?	☐	☐
13 Do you take work home?	☐	☐
14 Do you drink more than eight cups of caffeinated drinks (coffee, tea, cola, chocolate) each day?	☐	☐
15 Do you show Type A Behaviour?	☐	☐

Scoring		Points
1 yes	score 20	_____
2 yes	score 10	_____
3 yes	score 5 (if you attend more than once a month score 10)	_____
4 yes	score 15	_____
5 yes	score 10	_____
6 yes	score 10	_____
7 yes	score 10	_____
8 yes	score 10 for each course attended	_____
9 yes	score 15	_____

Total score for good coping strategies: [ ]

10 yes	subtract 10 points for each pack of 20 cigarettes smoked each day	_____
11 yes	subtract 10 points for every eight units drunk each week above the recommended limits; 21 units for women and 28 units for men	_____
12 yes	subtract 10	_____
13 yes	subtract 5 points for each night of the week that you take work home	_____
14 yes	subtract 5 points for every five cups over eight cups per day	_____
15 yes	check your Type A Behaviour assessment. Subtract 5 points if you scored between 40 and 60; 10 points if you scored 60 to 70 and 15 points if you scored over 70	_____

Total score for poor coping strategies: [ ]

Coping ability score: Subtract your score for poor coping strategies from your score for good coping strategies: [ ]

Evaluation

A positive score indicates you have good coping ability –
the higher your score the better your ability to deal with the
pressures and demands you face.

A negative score indicates you have poor coping ability –
the lower your score the lower your ability to deal with the
pressures and demands you face.

YOUR COPING ABILITY

Items 1 to 9 can help you deal with pressures and demands when
practised regularly. If you answered yes to items 10 to 15 then you
may be using these strategies to deal with pressures and demands but in
the long run they could be a threat to your health.

List your most commonly practised coping strategies:

GOOD COPING STRATEGIES (Items 1 to 9)	POOR COPING STRATEGIES (Items 10 to 15)
_____	_____
_____	_____
_____	_____
_____	_____
_____	_____

Use these lists to focus your attention on developing
appropriate and effective coping strategies.

To deal with stress effectively, you must adjust your
stress balance to keep it in and around the normal zone. This
means not going too far and too often into the distress zone
and making it easier to enter and remain in the eustress zone
when the need arises. Getting the right balance is achieved by
adjusting the weight in the pans. Clearly there are two ways
in which this can be done: either by altering demands or by
improving coping ability (Figure 9).

Change unhealthy coping strategies for good healthy
coping strategies.

When the balance tips into the distress zone (perceived
demands outweigh perceived ability to cope), adjustments can

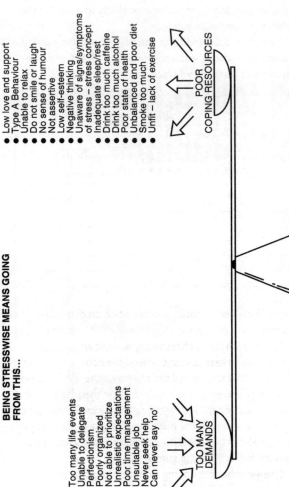

BEING STRESSWISE MEANS GOING FROM THIS...

- Too many life events
- Unable to delegate
- Perfectionism
- Poorly organized
- Not able to prioritize
- Unrealistic expectations
- Poor time management
- Unsuitable job
- Never seek help
- Can never say 'no'

TOO MANY DEMANDS

- Low love and support
- Type A Behaviour
- Unable to relax
- Do not smile or laugh
- No sense of humour
- Not assertive
- Low self-esteem
- Negative thinking
- Unaware of signs/symptoms of stress – stress concept
- Inadequate sleep/rest
- Drink too much caffeine
- Drink too much alcohol
- Poor state of health
- Unbalanced and poor diet
- Smoke too much
- Unfit – lack of exercise

POOR COPING RESOURCES

Figure 9 Factors altering demand and ability to cope.

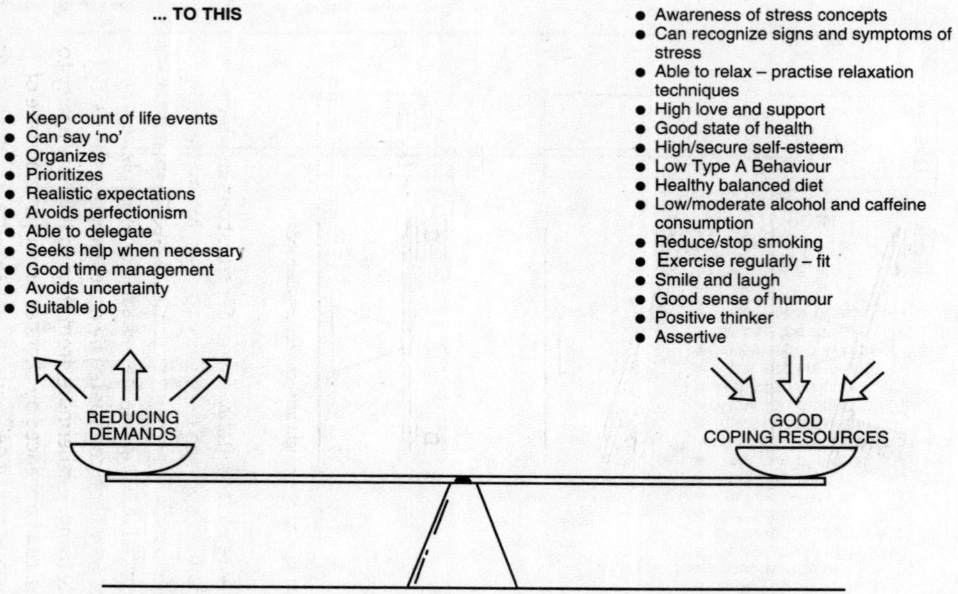

... TO THIS

- Keep count of life events
- Can say 'no'
- Organizes
- Prioritizes
- Realistic expectations
- Avoids perfectionism
- Able to delegate
- Seeks help when necessary
- Good time management
- Avoids uncertainty
- Suitable job

REDUCING DEMANDS

- Awareness of stress concepts
- Can recognize signs and symptoms of stress
- Able to relax – practise relaxation techniques
- High love and support
- Good state of health
- High/secure self-esteem
- Low Type A Behaviour
- Healthy balanced diet
- Low/moderate alcohol and caffeine consumption
- Reduce/stop smoking
- Exercise regularly – fit
- Smile and laugh
- Good sense of humour
- Positive thinker
- Assertive

GOOD COPING RESOURCES

Figure 9 (contd.) Factors altering demand and ability to cope.

be made to reduce demands (Figure 10) or to build up coping resources so that the balance swings back into the normal zone.

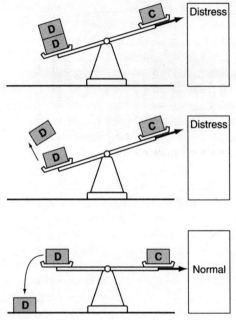

Figure 10 Getting the right balance: reducing demands

We will inevitably encounter situations in which demands outweigh our ability to cope. No matter how much our coping resources are increased, demands have the potential of being one step ahead. For example, it is certain that we will be confronted by novel situations as part of daily living. Furthermore, from time to time our ability to cope can be reduced by changes in our general state of health, allowing demands to get the better of us when we are not feeling so good.

Normally we would not have given these demands a second thought. Nevertheless, building up your coping resources so you have plenty of reserve will enable you to deal with extra and taxing demands without tipping your balance too far into the distress zone (Figure 11).

Building up your coping resources will make it easier for you to enter and operate in the eustress zone.

Adjusting your balance in this way is achieved by preparing yourself to keep one step ahead of 'reasonable' demands by learning skills to build up your coping resources. For most of the time this will keep you in the normal zone but with a season ticket to enter the eustress zone. However, additional and excessive demands will inevitably arise and tax our ability to cope. So increasing your coping reserves will help lessen the blow and keep you away from the depths of the distress zone – avoiding the bad and ugly!

Ironically, under some circumstances, thinking we have too much ability to cope can also cause distress. This can occur in two ways. First, when the perceived demands may be too few and consequently do not balance our perceived ability to cope. We can then feel under-used; we feel we have the ability to do more and our skills and expertise are not being utilized. Clearly, it is not appropriate to say to someone in this situation, 'Go away and reduce your coping reserves to match your level of demand'. The right balance is achieved by increasing demands (Figure 12).

Second, if we have unrealistic views of our abilities to handle demands, we may perceive that we can cope with more and more when in fact we cannot. To avoid tipping the balance into the distress zone, we must be realistic about our expectations thus reviewing our ability to cope.

Adjusting the balance is a continuous operation of altering demands and coping resources. You are the only person who can adjust your stress balance.

Keeping your balance right can be achieved by learning skills to reduce or increase demands and by building up coping resources.

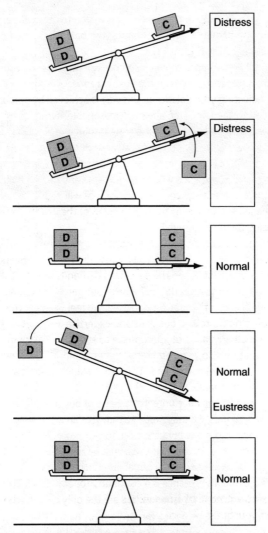

Figure 11 Getting the right balance: building up coping resources.

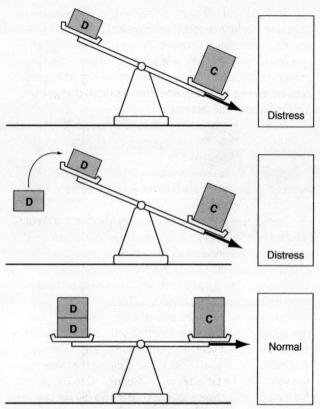

Figure 12 Getting the right balance: increasing demands.

Reducing demands

Keep count of life events

Too many changes in a relatively short period can tax your ability to adapt, resulting in distress and ill health.

To avoid this problem, always keep an eye on your number of life change events. Use the life events list as a checklist and keep a tally of your score.

Try to prevent too many of these events occurring in a short time. So, for example, if you have just changed jobs, moved house to an area miles from your family and friends and taken on a mortgage, it would be wise to postpone other plans or projects until you have settled. If you are nearing retirement, consider making a gradual rather than a sudden change from full-time work to full retirement.

Traumatic life events, such as divorce, serious illness or death of a loved one, are likely to reduce your coping reserves. This will make you more vulnerable to the dangers of distress. At such times it would be wise to consider the number of demands you are dealing with and to build up your coping resources through love and support.

The life events list is by no means exhaustive. You should identify events in your life which require an adjustment in order for you to handle them. These can be pleasant as well as unpleasant events. Give each a score according to your judgement of how they compare with the events and scores shown on the life events scale.

For each and every one of us, there is a one in ten chance (ten per cent risk) that we will suffer a serious illness during the next two years. But your life events score during the previous year may increase your risk of ill health during the following two years (see the table below). So scoring 150 to 299 points will increase your chance to about one in two (50 per cent risk). This may be a result of excessive cortisol release since many life events require attention over a relatively long period. Under these circumstances, cortisol can reduce our ability to fight infection and makes us more susceptible to disease.

Score	Risk of illness during next two years
300 or more	80%
150–299	50%
100–149	30%
less than 100	no change in risk

Note that the life events scale is based on studies of many thousands of people, so this scale is not very accurate in predicting the illness vulnerability of individuals. This is because each of us will perceive the events differently and the ability to cope with them will vary considerably from individual to individual. Nonetheless, it is wise to consider the effects on our health and performance of accumulating stressors.

Learn to say 'no'

Some people find it very difficult to say 'no' to requests from friends and work colleagues, even though they feel unable to cope with more work. They often feel it is a sign of lack of cooperation or an admission that they cannot handle their work. They feel that refusing to help may prejudice their promotion prospects or affect their relationship with others.

More work here does not just mean work connected with our jobs but also requests to join another fund-raising event, coach the local football team, service the car, decorate the house and so on. As the saying goes, 'If you want something doing, always ask a busy person because they are usually the ones who are unable to say 'no'!'

If you feel you cannot take on more work then be honest, clear and assertive in your reply. Point out how much you are currently doing and what is waiting to be done, or that there are circumstances in your domestic life making it difficult for you to work extra hours.

It is important that you say 'no' in the right way. Julie, a secretary, told us about her main source of stress at work. 'My boss always gives me a pile of work at around 4.00 p.m. and expects it to be completed before I finish work at 5.00 p.m. Sometimes I'm still typing at 6.00 p.m.' We asked why she had never said anything. 'I'm afraid he will think I'm not being cooperative and I might lose my job.'

We pointed out the consequences of her distress and suggested she asked her boss to prioritize the work in the following way. 'I realize that this work is important; however, I finish work at 5.00 p.m. and when you give me work at this time of the day I'm usually here until 6.00 p.m. I have an important appointment tonight so I would appreciate it if you would kindly sort out those items that are urgent and I'll make sure they are done before I leave. I will come in early tomorrow morning and deal with the rest.'

So what happened when Julie tried this way of saying, 'No, I'm not prepared to tackle all those demands'? Mr Smith did just as she asked. In fact, he designated only two letters as urgent. Julie left work at 5.00 p.m. and tells us that she has only worked later than that on two occasions since. Julie's response was assertive. She stated her case clearly and honestly, was firm and polite and suggested what might be done to help resolve the situation. Being assertive will help you say 'no' in the right way.

Whatever the situation or circumstance, one thing is certain: if you take on more than you feel able to handle, then you are likely to feel pressured, harassed and rushed, and your performance will suffer. Jobs will take longer to do and may not be done well. So saying 'no' and seeking clarification of priorities, planning ahead and being realistic about what you can achieve makes sense in the long run.

Organize your life, prioritize and be realistic about what you can achieve

Some people find it helpful to plan ahead: from day to day, week to week, month to month and year to year. Others have the philosophy of 'live for today' which reminds us not to be too obsessed with rigidly organizing the future. However, even carefree people must plan ahead in some way or another. This should include setting priorities and being realistic about what can be achieved.

Setting realistic goals

Many unnecessary demands can result from setting unrealistic goals which are difficult to attain. This is particularly true for Type As. Being realistic about what you can achieve will reduce demands. This will mean being honest about your abilities. Winning promotion to a job you have always wanted but find you cannot handle is one of the major sources of distress.

To set your priorities and realistic goals, take a piece of paper and write your objectives and goals in life.

Now, for each item identify the importance you attach to it. Grade the importance by using five stars for top priority and one star for the least. Now go through the list again and mark those items that you feel you can realistically achieve with an 'R' or highlighter pen. Delete those items which you feel are too difficult to attain or are unattainable. Now sit back and review your list. You may need to decide on a timescale for some items – what your goals are for the next month, year and so on. Construct a short-term and long-term plan. You will probably realize that many of your goals are achievable simply through minor changes in your lifestyle, perhaps devoting a little more time to one area rather than another.

By undertaking this exercise you are planning your life, prioritizing your activities and being realistic about what you might achieve. In this way you will have more chance of fulfilling your expectations. When expectations are achieved, self-esteem is high and this will enable you to deal more effectively with stress. Frequent failure to achieve unrealistic goals severely damages self-esteem and opens the door to aggression or depression.

Clearly, circumstances change, so you will need to update your lifeplan regularly, maybe weekly or monthly. You may find it an interesting exercise to construct your lifeplan at this stage of the book and again when you have finished reading it.

Organizing and prioritizing

Planning and prioritizing your work can help you reduce and avoid distress.

Much anxiety can build up if the tasks that need to be completed seem never-ending. We start to wonder how and when to fit in other essential activities. Look at your work schedule, prioritize and plan the order of completion, considering deadlines and importance. It is not much use spending a lot of time and effort on minor tasks, and perhaps getting tired and irritated, when more important and urgent jobs need to be completed, and done well. Try to concentrate on one task at a time, particularly if this is a major and important one.

One man described to us how he dealt with his office letters, memos, reports and so on. 'I start reading a document on the top of the pile of papers on my desk. I get halfway through and my mind wanders to a letter I caught a glimpse of halfway down the pile. I can't resist leaving the document I'm reading to pull out the letter. I start reading the letter, think 'Yes I must do this, that or the other' and then push it to one side. I go back to the first document and, having lost my train of thought, I start at the beginning. Soon I'm off into the pile again. As a result I don't seem to get things done very quickly and end up thinking and worrying about several things at the same time!'

Our advice to this man was to prioritize: Sort quickly through your papers and put them in order of importance. Make three piles and colour-code them: very urgent (green – go), urgent (amber – get ready) and not urgent (red – stop). Work through each pile in turn, dealing with the very urgent before proceeding to the urgent and so on. Of course, priorities can change so the order should not be considered fixed.

Wading through a sea of papers is one of today's worst office stressors. You can check your efficiency and your need to prioritize by ticking the corner of a document each time you read or look at it. You may be surprised at the number of ticks some documents accumulate.

Keeping a diary and appointment book is a very effective way of organizing yourself.

Write as much information as is appropriate about appointments, deadlines and reminders as they arise, for both work and home life. You will need a large enough diary to provide the space for notes and suggestions and drawing up plans for the day and week but this does not mean buying an additional briefcase to hold your 'mega-diary'! In this way you will have less need to make notes on scraps of paper which may get lost. Everything is in one place and time is not wasted wading through piles of notes. Give a high priority to personal and domestic problems since failure to deal with these will inevitably affect your work.

A well-maintained diary will help to reduce the worry and anxiety of wondering whether you will remember all your appointments. Make time every day to work with your diary. Use self-adhesive coloured dots or highlighter pens to prioritize tasks. Keep to the same colour for a specific activity: purple for deadlines, blue for meetings, yellow for telephone calls, for instance.

Avoid creating unnecessary deadlines and cluttering up your calendar with appointments.

An important factor in planning and setting priorities is being realistic about what can be achieved. If you are asked to give a time for completion of a task, do not put yourself under unnecessary pressure by saying next week (just to make yourself look efficient) when you know you may not meet that deadline.

Avoid perfectionism

Perfectionists in particular need to be realistic. Type As are bugged by perfectionism. Always striving obsessively to achieve perfection is usually counter-productive. Many perfectionists believe that if perfection is not achieved, disaster is bound to result. It must be realized that the 'perfect and best' result can only be achieved once in a lifetime. Striving to better your best performance each time leads to unnecessary demands, pressures, distress and feelings of failure if it is not achieved.

Settle for your best effort and be content with what you have done.

You probably will have produced a good and satisfactory job without ending up distressed.

Perfectionism as described here should not be confused with working conscientiously and diligently to achieve your best performance and good results, particularly where it is essential for tasks to be done correctly. So getting rid of perfectionism does not mean attending less to your work and making mistakes or producing poor performance. We describe perfectionists as those people who are obsessive about producing a 100 per cent absolutely correct piece of work in everything they do.

Why do perfectionists strive for perfection? We asked a self-confessed perfectionist to tell us about the advantages of perfectionism. She said, 'It sometimes produces an excellent piece of work which pleases me very much.' 'Are there any disadvantages?' we asked. She thought for a while and replied, 'Yes I suppose there are. I often worry about not doing a good job. This means I usually stick to techniques I know well so I hardly ever experiment with new ideas. I am self-critical, set myself high standards, get very upset if things are not turning out the way I want them to. Sometimes I spend such an incredible amount of time trying to produce a perfect result that I become agitated. Usually I end up settling for what I had achieved in the first place. In the meantime, I waste a lot of time and feel annoyed with myself.'

Another key factor in planning and prioritizing is managing time. Learning the skills to manage your time effectively can reduce demands and increase coping ability, thus helping tip your stress balance into the eustress zone. Some aspects of time management are dealt with in the section on modifying and reducing Type A Behaviour.

Delegate

Another way of reducing demands at home and work is to delegate. If you are in a position to delegate at work then you have undoubtedly demonstrated that you are good at your job and you are probably managing, supervising and directing others. There can be a tendency for you to believe (particularly if you are Type A) that jobs will get done better and quicker if you do them all yourself, but this is often not the case. You can become overloaded with tasks which could be delegated to someone else.

When you delegate, make sure you choose the person best suited to the job and who has the time to devote to it. Give clear instructions and information about what you expect and reassure the person of your confidence in them and that you will be available should they need any advice or assistance.

There are many positive benefits to delegating. Giving responsibility to another person makes them feel part of what is going on, that you have confidence and trust in them, and it provides them with the experience they will need for their career advancement. Their self-esteem is boosted and they will probably perform well with their stress balance in the eustress zone.

Individuals can often face a mountain of demands if they have multiple roles. Looking after the home or family, planning or preparing meals, shopping, cleaning etc. This job is frequently combined with employment outside the home. Clearly, reducing demands by delegating domestic duties can help avoid distress.

Seek help when the going gets tough

Seeking help and support from others in the tasks you perform can be mutually beneficial in reducing workload and demands. Rather than struggle, ask for help. Struggling on your own can be very distressful and will certainly make a task more difficult to complete.

It is better to admit you need help with a demand and then go on to satisfactorily complete it, than to struggle on your own to end up producing a poor piece of work, or even failing to complete it.

Find a job which suits your personality and abilities

If you are looking for a job, you should seek one which you feel suits your personality, skills and ability. If you are already in a stressful job, then review the demands placed upon you and your abilities to handle them. Consider your work expectations and be realistic about your ability to achieve them.

Learn to work effectively

Many aspects of your work may be decided by your employer or organization, leaving you with little control over what you do. In situations where this is distressful, stand back and ask yourself whether the demands and pressures are real and reasonable or whether your perceived lack of control is a result of your unrealistic expectations.

Clearly, the physical conditions of your work environment are important, not least from a safety point of view: bad lighting, insufficient heating, poor ventilation, noise, overcrowding, lack of privacy and uncomfortable office furniture are frequent sources of dissatisfaction, frustration and distress. Many employers appreciate that the right physical environment will encourage productivity and creativity, so you should not be hesitant about approaching your employer if you feel these things are causing you distress. There are some changes you can probably make for yourself such as brightening your immediate work area with coloured posters, postcards, photographs, cartoons and plants.

There is much you can do to organize your work. Take short breaks from routine tasks even if it means simply closing your eyes for a few minutes and relaxing. Practise a relaxation technique (such as those described below) at your desk or bench. Arrange your office or surroundings so you have to get up and walk to the filing cabinet or to answer the telephone. When you talk on the telephone, concentrate on the task in hand and do not polyphase (do more than one thing at a time). Be assertive, say 'no' when you feel overloaded with work. Seek immediate clarification about what is required when you are asked to do a job. At this stage you should point out any difficulties or problems you foresee and ask for help if necessary. It is always more difficult to do this after the event, though you can always go back and ask again. In the meantime, you may have worried unnecessarily over difficulties and problems.

If you have a lot to do, arrange your jobs in order of priority. It is usually most productive, effective and satisfying to complete one job at a time before moving on to the next.

Do not rush; spend some time thinking about how to tackle problems and plan your course of action. Routine jobs are often best tackled using a strict timetable such as opening mail first thing in the morning. Do not clutter your diary with appointments or make appointments when you know you may not be able or will be pushed to keep them. Leave some time for yourself during the day for relaxation and never miss your lunch and tea breaks. Use them effectively: get out of the work environment, go for a walk or relax and read a novel. Learn to manage your time effectively.

Most people work with others, so you should pay particular attention to giving and receiving support and building self-esteem with respect to your work. Learn the art of good communication and assertiveness. Develop the art of listening – you will not only learn more by listening rather than talking but you will form better relationships – people like to talk and tell you about themselves. Control your voice in discussions; do not become threatening or emotional. You will get your views over better by using clearly stated points in an assertive manner. Do not underestimate the value of good humour.

Avoid uncertainty

Worrying about 'what might happen if...' may be unnecessary. Find out the facts about things before you get anxious and panic. When you have collected as much information as you can, it might then be obvious that your initial fears and worries were ill-founded and you will have avoided unnecessary distress. On the other hand, if your worries were warranted you will be prepared and can plan all the possible alternatives and seek help if necessary. This will make you feel less uncertain. Coping with demands and pressures is easier if you know exactly what you are dealing with.

Increasing demands

There are a number of situations where an individual may feel that there are too few demands in their life: too little stimulation and not enough challenges. They feel they have the capacity to handle more. They feel under-used, bored and frustrated. Self-esteem suffers, motivation declines and eventually performance becomes poor in all they do.

One situation where this may arise is retirement. This can involve a sudden change from active and busy full-time work to a less demanding life with few deadlines to keep. As a retired person, you can experience an overnight change from being an important part of an organization and making a valuable contribution to society, to a position where your usefulness within society seems diminished. It is not possible to reduce your perceived coping ability to match your lower perceived demands, so you should take on new demands. Maybe take up a hobby, join an evening class and learn something that you always wanted to do but never had the time for while working. Plan and do the things you did not have the time for, such as taking a long trip abroad. Keep up and renew friendships, become involved in community projects, local clubs and voluntary organizations. Plan your day as if it were a working day; build in time for domestic duties, shopping, walking, hobbies, and so on. But beware – do not increase demands to the point where your stress balance tips into the distress zone.

Another situation where too few demands lead to distress is where an employee feels their abilities and skills are not adequately used. The remedy is to ask the employer for more work. On the other hand, it may be that someone in this position is in the wrong job. Finding the right job to suit your aptitude and abilities is not an easy task. Where there is a significant mismatch, distress inevitably results. Correcting this situation may mean requesting the organization to reappraise the job role with a view to moving you to a different job or it may mean leaving the job and seeking one which is more suitable.

We can find ourselves in a position of having too few demands if we lose our job, face a change in family situation when children leave home or our partner dies. When we get back on our feet it may be necessary to increase demands in a similar way to the retirement situation described above.

Learning to relax

Recharge your batteries

A period of relaxation is a time to recharge your batteries. When you are relaxed, your noradrenaline, adrenaline and cortisol levels are lowered and your body activity is opposite to that experienced during the activation of the stress response. Heart rate and breathing decrease and the body feels warm due to dilation of the blood vessels. Sweating decreases, saliva secretion increases, muscle tension decreases, and the mind feels settled. However, your body is always ready to respond to danger within a split second even from a deep state of relaxation.

Develop relaxing daily activities

There are a number of specific procedures that bring about a state of relaxation, for example yoga, meditation, progressive and deep muscular relaxation, autogenics, self-hypnosis and biofeedback. Many of these procedures must be learned and practised regularly.

Practising a relaxation technique should become part of your life – just as brushing your teeth twice a day, you should actively relax every day, and not just when you are feeling or expect to feel stressed.

Learning these techniques takes time and you should not expect too much too soon. Furthermore, it can take a while before the benefits are experienced but the results are worth waiting for. Below we describe the techniques we use and take you through the procedures so you can learn to achieve a state of relaxation.

There are also a number of activities that can be built into your daily routine to make you feel relaxed and revitalized. Taking a hot bubble bath, floating in a swimming pool, taking a steam bath, sauna or jacuzzi can bring about a state of relaxation. So too can going for a pleasant walk, taking a weekend break away from home, listening to your favourite music (Baroque music appears to be particularly effective), reading your favourite books, a night out at the theatre, an evening meal at your favourite restaurant.

Massage is a particularly effective way of relaxing the muscles which in turn leads to a calm mind. Also taking up a hobby, a leisure activity, joining a club, tinkering with the car, tackling a DIY project or developing new interests can all be relaxing as long as they are looked on as relaxation activities. But beware, some of these activities can be stressful if tackled in the wrong way.

A well-planned holiday of at least a week's duration is a good way to recharge your batteries. However, take heed, even a holiday can be packed full of distress. There might be airport delays, language and currency problems and there could be plenty of rain instead of 'guaranteed' sun. Stomach trouble can strike, you get sunburnt, and your partner forgot to pack your favourite beachwear. What is intended to be a relaxing holiday can turn into a distressful nightmare! Preparation and planning can help avoid many of these problems and minimize distress.

Quieting reflex – QR

Step one	Close your eyes. Pinpoint in your mind what is annoying or stressing you.
Step two	Say to yourself, 'Alert mind, calm body. I'm not going to let this get to me.'
Step three	Smile to yourself. You can practise smiling to yourself without showing a smile on your face. In this way, your smile will not be obvious to others around you.

Step four	Breathe in to the count of three while imagining that the air comes in through holes in your feet. Feel the sensation of warmth and heaviness flowing throughout your body, starting at your feet and ending at your head.
Step five	Breathe out to the count of three. Visualize your breath passing through your body from your head and out through the holes in your feet. Feel the warmth and heaviness flow through your body. Let your muscles relax, let the jaw, tongue and shoulders go limp.

Now open your eyes and resume your normal activity.

Relaxation should not be regarded as something done only outside work. Taking your regular coffee and lunch breaks is important; these are times for you to recharge your batteries. Try to get away from your office or work surroundings. Go for a short walk or read a favourite book. If you feel stressed during the day, sit back for a few minutes and practise a quick relaxation technique. Try the quieting reflex (QR). It takes only a few seconds and with practice achieves a body state opposite to activation of the alarm reaction.

With practice over several months, QR becomes automatic. It provides a pause for you to decide whether or not to stay stressed, tense and annoyed or to shift into a less irritated and more relaxed state.

Progressive and deep muscular relaxation

In this technique, each of the main groups of muscles is tensed then relaxed (progressive muscle relaxation – PMR). At each stage the mind is concentrated first on the feelings of tension and then on relaxation. With practice, you can learn to be aware of muscle tenseness so you can easily and automatically convert tension into relaxation. For example, many drivers find their shoulders hunched and hands gripping the steering wheel so tightly that the knuckles turn white. Through PMR, you will recognize this tension and automatically relax the muscles, thus reducing head, neck, shoulder and back pains and stiffness.

When the body muscles are relaxed, the mind relaxes and this reduces sympathetic nerve activity, leading to a decrease in heart rate and blood pressure. However, the technique is not recommended for sufferers with high blood pressure (hypertension). This is because the tensing of the muscles causes elevation of the blood pressure which then decreases when the muscles are relaxed. So if you suffer with hypertension it is not wise to increase your blood pressure further by tensing the muscles during PMR. Instead we advise you to practise deep muscular relaxation (DMR). This technique is similar to PMR but the muscles are not deliberately tensed prior to relaxing.

You will need to find a suitable place to practise these techniques: somewhere quiet and warm, where you will not be disturbed. It is advisable not to try them for up to two hours after eating a heavy meal, and use a firm, upright chair rather than an armchair, which can encourage drowsiness. It is helpful to get someone to read the procedure to you so you can concentrate on the movements and technique. Alternatively, ask someone with a soft, relaxing voice to record the instructions (we have deliberately written them almost as a commentary) and play the recording or CD back to yourself. A pre-recorded CD of these procedures is available from *Stresswise* at www.stresswise.com.

Meditation

Whereas PMR and DMR concentrate on muscle relaxation, meditation concentrates on relaxing the mind. The technique is straightforward. The mind is focused for 20 minutes on a word or sound, known as a focal device. This is repeated over and over again in the mind. As the technique is performed, thoughts will pass in and out of the mind. When the mind wanders it can be brought back to the focal device. With practice, the mind will wander less often as the repetition of the word engages the left side of the brain in a meaningless task. This side of the brain deals more with logical and analytical thinking and normally dominates our consciousness. When the word is repeated over and over again the left brain is occupied in the monotonous task of attending to the repetitious information. As this happens, the activity of the right side of the brain takes over. This side of the brain is involved with intuition, imagination and creativity. Suppressing the analytic activity of the left brain and allowing intuitive dominance of the right brain results in a reduction in stress response activation and an increase in tranquillity; a feeling of serenity.

During meditation, the body's oxygen requirement drops, the heart and breathing slow, blood pressure decreases. In fact, a general state of relaxation is achieved. Recordings of brainwave activity show more alpha rhythms which are characteristic of a state of relaxation.

There are a variety of meditation methods, but the basic technique is a very effective and beneficial relaxation tool which can be used by everyone.

The benefits of relaxation

Your coping abilities usually increase, making it likely that you will experience eustress rather than distress. However, there are a number of other benefits. Some doctors now use relaxation methods, particularly PMR, DMR and meditation, to treat patients with high blood pressure and high blood cholesterol, sometimes without the use of medication. In the same way that blood pressure and cholesterol levels rise as sympathetic arousal increases, so levels drop when sympathetic activity declines. Patients practising relaxation for one month or more have shown a decrease in blood cholesterol and other blood fats.

It has been reported that regular meditators make fewer visits to their doctors than non-meditators, and that a variety of physical ailments can be alleviated through meditation. While teaching relaxation techniques, we have seen some remarkable changes in our students. A 38-year-old woman with Raynaud's disease (painful cold fingers due to constriction of the digital arteries) reported that the condition disappeared two weeks after she learned to meditate. Three years later, she has not experienced the symptoms again. We have taught many people with sleep problems to meditate. In most cases their problems have disappeared within a week or two of starting meditation. A woman on tranquillizers managed to reduce her dose under the supervision of her doctor after we taught her to meditate. It must be said that these problems might have disappeared anyway or that it was not the meditation itself but the care and attention given to these people that did the trick. Maybe so, we cannot prove otherwise, but there is enough evidence to support the belief that the biological consequences of meditation can bring about such changes. A number of studies and surveys also support this view.

Other benefits of relaxation, and particularly of meditation, are increased mental alertness, improved concentration, creativity and memory, leading to better performance and enhanced or improved relationships. Regular practice can lead to improved wellbeing and a different, more rational attitude and view of life.

5

modifying Type A Behaviour

Type As, through their beliefs, attitudes and habits, frequently perceive situations as threatening and challenging when no real threat or challenge exists.

Research shows that one way in which children learn to behave in this manner is by copying their parents.

A child's upbringing can result in Type A Behaviour from an early age. If parents fail to provide unconditional love or set never-ending standards and expectations, the child's self-worth and self-esteem diminishes. At school, the child seizes any opportunity to perform well to boost their low self-esteem. Soon, self-worth and self-esteem become measured by achievements, particularly where it is believed these are admired by others. The struggle to achieve and to secure control over their environment continues into adult life, especially in their career, because the individual has learned to behave in a way that can be self-destructive in the long run.

But if Type A Behaviour is learned, then it can be *unlearned*.

Unlearning Type A Behaviour

Reduction of your Type A Behaviour can be achieved only by examining your beliefs, attitudes and habits; those habits with which you have burdened your life. A chronic sense of time urgency or a tendency to become easily upset and angry over trivia must be discarded or modified. To do this you must substitute new, healthy beliefs for your bad, unhealthy ones. The objective for treating Type A Behaviour is to change Anger, Irritation, Aggravation and Impatience (AIAI) into Acceptance (of the errors of yourself and of others), Serenity, Affection and Self-esteem enhancement (ASAS).

There are a number of ways of tackling this and they all take time to learn and practise; there is no quick way to unlearn or modify what has taken years to learn.

Drilling

As a start, set yourself drills aimed to make you do the opposite to what you normally do. For example, if you get impatient while waiting, then your drill would be to find a queue and practise waiting without getting impatient. Keep a paperback with you to read or a pack of postcards to write to friends or to make notes or plans for a DIY project. You might say avoiding queues is the best answer. Yes, but, being realistic, you cannot get through life these days without queuing at some time or another. If you travel by car you will certainly get caught in traffic jams. In this case, take the opportunity to relax; put the gear in neutral, handbrake on, feet on floor, breathe deeply and slowly, and recall a pleasant memory.

Review your driving habits – do you drive fast? Race the red light? Do a Grand Prix start on green? Overtake and weave in and out of traffic? If so, then set yourself drills such as driving mainly in the slow lane and keeping to one lane.

Make a list of your Type A behaviours using the description of Type A provided in Chapter 3, then make a diary of drills appropriate for your treatment. For example:

Monday: Speak more slowly.

Tuesday: Tackle one task/thing at a time (instead of polyphasing).

Wednesday: Keep mainly in the slow traffic lane (instead of weaving from one lane to another to get in the fastest moving lane).

Thursday: Walk more slowly.

Friday: Linger at the table (instead of rushing away as soon as you finish eating).

Saturday: Seek a long queue and practise waiting patiently (instead of getting impatient and irritated).

Sunday: Leave your watch off and practise being less time urgent (instead of letting time dictate your day).

Each day, concentrate on the specified drill. So for Monday, concentrate on speaking more slowly; for Tuesday do only one task at a time, and so on. Gradually, with regular drilling, you replace your old Type A behaviours with new Type B behaviours. After a while these will become a habit in just the same way as you learned your Type A behaviours which formed your old habits. Without noticing, you will soon be practising Type B behaviours each day of the week and not only on your specified drill day.

Accept that your change from Type A towards Type B will take a long time to achieve. You will find it useful to construct a drill diary for each day of the year.

Cueing

To help you modify your Type A Behaviour use self-adhesive red hearts available from *Stresswise* at www.stresswise.com

which remind you to practise your drills. As an alternative to the hearts, you can use small self-adhesive coloured paper dots available from stationers. Place one in the centre of your watch face on the glass as a reminder to rid yourself of your chronic sense of time urgency. Every time you glance at your watch remember your drills.

Place a heart on your steering wheel or dashboard as a reminder to rid yourself of Type A driving habits.

Place one on the telephone to act as a cue to tackle one task at a time and not to polyphase while speaking. How about one on your placemat at the dinner table reminding you to eat more slowly and to linger at the table?

A heart paperclip (also available from *Stresswise*) can be used as a cue in your diary. It will remind you to slow down, not to clutter your day with appointments, to avoid creating unnecessary deadlines and to leave some time in the day for yourself.

We deliberately use hearts as cueing devices because of the associations between Type A Behaviour and the heart. Many participants in our stress management programmes find that this association, together with their awareness of the stress response and Type A Behaviour, motivates them more than anything else to modify their behaviour. As a typical example of this, a man related to us his experience while driving at the start of his counselling programme: 'I was sitting in the traffic jam staying in the slow lane but I could feel my noradrenaline start to flow. I looked at the heart on the steering wheel and reminded myself that the way I was feeling could allow noradrenaline to strike at my heart. A traffic jam is not worth dying for so I turned my cassette on, sat back and relaxed. It was interesting watching those ignorant of this fact gambling with their life in more ways than one!'

Monitoring

Regular drilling takes a great deal of willpower. You will find it helpful to ask family and friends to act as monitors. Explain to them what you are doing and ask them to monitor your progress. They can remind you to drill if you lapse into your old Type A ways. The wife of a man on our programme hummed *The A Team* television show theme tune each time her husband lapsed into his Type A ways. Your monitors may also suggest drills for Type A Behaviours you are unaware you possess; Type As are often blind to their own behaviour. Ask your monitors to read the section on Type A Behaviour and invite their comments on the way you behave. Be prepared to listen carefully to your monitor's observations. They can provide you with support and at the same time help themselves to modify their own Type A Behaviour.

Examining your beliefs

Alleviating your sense of time urgency and managing your time effectively

Question your Type A time urgent belief. Answer true or false to this statement: *'Being time urgent has helped me gain success'*.

If you answer 'true', then think carefully. How successful are you? It may be that any failures are a result of mistakes that could have been avoided if you had been patient and taken time to think and organize, to be creative and innovative. For this reason, some drills are designed to rid you of your haste; for example, eat, talk, walk, drive more slowly and avoid polyphasing.

Ask yourself if frantically switching traffic lanes gets you to work quicker. Carry on driving in your usual manner for the next week and time your journey each day. Then the following week, keep in one lane (where it is possible) and time your journeys. Now take the average journey time for each week. Most drivers find a difference in their journey time of only a few minutes. Now think: is it worth exposing your heart to potentially fatal levels of noradrenaline to save a few minutes each day?

Other drills are aimed to repair damage done by years of time urgency. Type As have little time to recall memories, so some time should be allocated to this activity. Review your life and plan ahead, setting realistic goals.

Years of struggling to do more and more in less time encourages the Type A individual to concentrate on achievements and strategies to gain or maintain control. There is little space in their lives for relaxation or cultural activities. To correct this, stop measuring your life in quantities – number of committees served on, amount of money earned, number of accomplishments, etc. Think instead in terms of quality of life. To help bring this about, your diary should include drills such as reading more (but not technical and financial texts or material associated with your job), visiting museums, art galleries, theatres and observing nature.

When we asked the wife of one of our Type A group participants if she had noticed any change in her husband's behaviour, she said, 'While we were driving in Wales, Peter commented on the beauty of the scenery. He never did this before the course. It may sound a small thing but when you spend all your time rushing about from A to B a change like this is noticeable.' Try taking off your watch; you will find that you have all the time in the world.

Take time to look around to see what pleasurable things can be found.

You will then rid yourself of your obsession with numbers and quantities and instead describe in words the beauty of things surrounding you.

Ask yourself: are you preoccupied with your own attempts to achieve your goals? Workaholics are blind to the fact that they are not giving time to their families. Even major events in the lives of their children go unnoticed. A recent survey of workaholics revealed some disturbing and sad indicators of this exclusive preoccupation with self and ambitions. A child drew a picture of his family: Mummy, sister and himself – but Daddy was missing. Another child waiting for his father at the airport was reported to have asked several men, 'Are you my daddy?' How often we have heard reformed Type As sadly express regret at missing so much of their children's development. The missed school sports, parents' evenings, nativity plays and so on. Once gone they cannot be replaced.

Learn how to manage your time effectively. Our lives are dominated by time and for Type As, time is more of a problem than others. We all know there are 24 hours in each day and we like to use our waking hours effectively. Nobody likes wasting time unnecessarily; it is in reality losing part of one's life. But if you become obsessed with time, the resultant distress could be shortening your life and certainly reducing its quality.

Managing your time effectively at work is important if you wish to avoid distress. The section on reducing demands suggested a number of ways in which you can do this by planning, prioritizing, setting realistic goals, being assertive, avoiding perfectionism, saying 'no' and delegating. You will also be more time-effective if you tackle jobs which require mental effort when you feel at your best and able to concentrate; in other words when you are in the eustress zone. Do the tasks requiring less mental effort when you are not able to concentrate as well or when you anticipate interruptions. Do not waste time worrying unnecessarily about future events. *Remember, it's not the hours you put in – it's what you put into the hours that counts*.

Balancing your time between family, leisure, work and sleep is important. Regularly spending long periods at work will inevitably mean less time for your family and for leisure activities. Too much work often leads to mental fatigue and difficulty in relaxing, which will inevitably affect the quality of the time spent with your family and friends. Finding time to spend with your partner, children, family and friends will enable you to nurture love and support and to enhance your self-esteem and happiness.

Include in your daily schedule periods for relaxation, exercise and time for you to spend on your own. Pamper yourself each day. Build 'idling time' into your routine so as not to rush the things you do. Allow plenty of time for washing, dressing and eating breakfast even if it means rising half an hour earlier in the morning. Spend time on meditation and muscular relaxation. Allow more time than you estimate for journeys and give yourself time to be punctual for appointments. In this way, you will reduce anxiety if you are unexpectedly delayed.

Remember, there are 168 hours in each week so there is time to devote to everything; sit down and plan how you want to spend your time. Time is precious and we all want to spend it happily. So remember, for every 60 seconds you are angry you lose a minute of happiness.

Alleviating your easily aroused anger and hostility

Question your Type A anger and hostility beliefs. Answer true or false to this statement: '*I need aggression and hostility to succeed*'. If your answer is 'true', then consider that by using aggression and hostility rather than understanding, you may damage your health and your relationships with family, friends and work colleagues. In the long run, this will not lead to success.

Making mistakes, failing to achieve goals, receiving adverse criticism, particularly in front of others, and perceiving a situation as unfair or embarrassing can trigger frustration and anger. As we described earlier, such emotion leads to excessive release of noradrenaline, the potential killer. When you next feel yourself getting irritated, aggravated and angry remember that, if triggered, your anger can inflict the most damage on the person you least intend – yourself. Train yourself to avoid anger: do not get hooked, practise anger control and use the quieting reflex.

Try these two techniques: avoiding the hook and anger control.

Avoiding the hook

Picture yourself as a fish in a river. Every morning you wake up and start swimming. The waters ahead appear clear but on the banks of the river are anglers casting their hooks, hoping to catch you. Suddenly a worm on a hook appears in front of you. The bait looks tempting but if you bite you will be hooked. Think: 'Bite or pass by?' You pass by, avoiding the bait. Unexpectedly another hook drops in front of you. Ask yourself; 'Bite or pass by?' You pass by, only to find more hooks appearing along your journey.

Type As bite all the time, perhaps 30 to 40 times a day. The problem is that we have no idea when the next hook is going to appear and this makes anger and hostility difficult to deal with.

If you take the bait you will get hooked!

Anger control

If you feel yourself starting to take the bait, then say 'stop'. Detach yourself from the situation and analyse your behaviour and feelings. Ask yourself, 'What provoked me?' Identify the causes of your anger and the beliefs, attitudes and feelings that led you to take the bait. Now replay the situation again in your mind to see whether the way in which you acted was appropriate, justified and rational. Usually you will find taking the bait serves no real purpose. Remain calm and hold a conversation with yourself (called 'self-talk'): 'It's not worth getting worked up about'; 'There is no real reason to argue'; 'Keep cool, don't take the bait'; 'Unpleasantness can lead to more unpleasantness'; 'Practise QR'; 'Reason it out'.

The trick is not to take the bait and therefore not to get angry in the first place. Do not get hooked into things you cannot do anything about. So if the train is delayed and you are late for your appointment, use self-talk to accept that there is nothing you can do to make up the lost time. Instead use your energy to think about alleviating the problem. When you arrive at the station, telephone your appointment, explain the situation and say you will be arriving as soon as possible. You also have little control over the errors and antics of others, so learn to accept their mistakes and trivialities. If you cannot, this will inevitably lead to frustration, anger and hostility.

Work at lessening your sense of time urgency. Impatience is a mild form of irritation which in turn is a mild form of anger. Above all, recognize that your anger and hostility are manifestations of your low self-esteem. When self-esteem is high, then anger and hostility will be low. Blows to your self-esteem will easily trigger hostility, so work toward enhancing your self-esteem and practise being assertive. Note that your self-esteem is affected by the degree of love and affection in your life, so when love and affection are present, self-esteem will be high and the potential for hostility will be low. Learning to give and receive love and affection is therefore vital in your battle against anger and hostility. Tell your partner and children how much you value their love, affection and support and express your feelings to them. Take an interest in your friends and share their ups and downs. Also, learn to laugh at yourself and your mistakes and errors. Stop taking yourself too seriously!

For once, it is better to be in the 'B' team rather than the 'A' team.

Finally

To deal with stress effectively you need to adjust your stress balance to keep it in and around the normal zone. This means not going too far and too often into the distress zone and making it easier to enter and remain in the eustress zone. Adjusting your stress balance also makes it easier to enter and remain in the eustress zone when the need arises. Getting the right balance is achieved by adjusting the contents in each pan by altering demands and/or by improving coping ability.

The way to achieve the right balance with the assistance of the scores from the questionnaires that you have completed is to quantify your signs and symptoms of stress and to identify your most significant stressors.

This will help you to select appropriate stress management techniques from the book to put into practice. This is a start to developing your own stress management plan to alter your demands and help with improving your coping ability.

Remember that this book on stress management is meant to act as a guide to help you focus on particular aspects of your circumstances that you may not have otherwise considered. Most of our distress results from our interactions with others. We cannot prescribe individual tailor-made solutions. Each of us has to work on our own stress management plan according to our own individual situations.

We wish you success in managing stress and being wise about your stress.

Notes

Notes

Notes